IRISH
PLACENAMES

A Paperback Original
First published 1990 by
Poolbeg Press
Knocksedan House
Swords Co Dublin

ISBN 1 85371 087 3

Cover design by Pomphrey Associates
Printed and bound in Great Britain by
The Guernsey Press Co. Ltd., Guernsey, Channel Islands.

The Poolbeg Book of
IRISH
PLACENAMES
Sean McMahon

POOLBEG

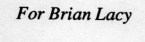

For Brian Lacy

Contents

Munster

Ulster

Introduction

We've come to the crossroads. Come here and look at it, man!
Look at it! And we call that crosswords Tobair Vree. And why do
we call it Tobair Vree? I'll tell you why. Tobair means a well. But
what does Vree mean? It's a corruption of Brian—an erosion of
Tobair Bhriain. Beacuse a hundred-and-fifty years ago there used
to be a well there, not at the crossroads, mind you—that would be
too simple—but in a field close to the crossroads. And an old man
called Brian, whose face was disfigured by an enormous growth,
got it into his head that the water in that well was blessed; and every
day for seven months he went there and bathed his face in it. But
the growth did not go away; and one morning Brian was found
drowned in that well. And ever since that crossroads is known as
Tobair Vree—even though that well has long since dried up.

This quotation from Brian Friel's superb play *Translations*
gives some idea of the fascination and complexity of Irish
placenames. They are often the oldest pieces of the Irish
language remaining alive in a district and in many cases the
only ones. (Orangemen from the Shankill Road or Bally-
hackamore on their way to Finaghy or Edenderry are on the
whole not aware that these are Gaelic names.) Sometimes
religion had a hand in the making of the name, as in Killybegs
or Desertmartin; sometimes the armed defender, as in Rath-
keltar or Lisbaby; sometimes the namer was a joker, as in
Tandragee; sometimes, perhaps very often, he was a poet, as
in Glenagivney.

1

One poet, John Montague, summarises the situation in the lines

> All around, shards of a lost tradition.
> From the Rough Field I went to school
> in the Glen of the Hazels....

This elegant tribute to the magic meanings locked in the placenames Garvaghey and Glencull is what this little book is about. The stepping-stone between the residual name and its meaning is the Gaelic name preserved in oral tradition and given here in modern Irish and standard spelling for consistency. When the Normans came to make their conquest of Ireland, unfortunately for Ireland a very pale effort at conquest, they continued the Scandinavian practice of fresh-naming or modifying what they found. This modification (to use no more vituperative term) was continued by the British who took the names and rendered them into barely passable phonetic equivalents. The result was that root words, at least construable in the original Gaelic, became lost or buried through elision, compression or imperfect hearing. The effect has been to make the study of Irish placenames an excessively difficulty and teasing pursuit.

The great source work on the subject in modern times is the three-volume *Irish Names of Places* written by Patrick Weston Joyce. He was born in Co Limerick in 1827 and the work was published in 1869, 1875 and 1914, the year of his death. His work would have been impossible without the reports of the Ordnance Survey of the 1830s done by O'Curry and O'Donovan. He was a grammarian and a fluent Gaelic speaker who resisted fiercely the erosion of Irish. His pioneering work has largely been confirmed by modern scholarship but he was a typically romantic nineteenth-century scholar who had neither the scientific resources available to researchers today nor the heart always to resist colourful local derivations. He sums up the difficulties in the introduction to his first volume:

> This is the first book ever written on the subject. In this respect I am somewhat in the position of a settler in a new country who has all the advantages of priority of claim but who purchases them dearly, perhaps, by the labour and difficulty of breaking his way through the wilderness and clearing his settlement from primaeval forest and tangled undergrowth.

Even he could not have realised just how tangled the undergrowth really was. As one of the leading modern scholars on the subject, the late Deirdre Flanagan, has shown, notably in an article entitled "Exemplary Guide to the Study of a Placename," (*Ulster Local Studies*, November 1976). She takes the town of Glenavy in Co Antrim and discloses for it twenty-nine different documentary references, each with a different form of the name, from *Iathrach-Patricc* in the ninth-century *Book of Armagh* to "Lenavy" in 1615. The correct name in modern Irish is *Lann Abhaigh* (the church/monastery of the dwarf), the traditional account of its source being that St Patrick left a certain Daniel in charge of his foundation. He was called "angel" because of his sanctity and "dwarf" because of his small stature. As she notes the element "glen" is peculiarly misleading because of the presence near the town of a recognisable valley.

Such meticulous research is beyond the scope or the interest of the average tourist. It is simply an indication of the difficulty and the fascination of what is called *dinnsean-chas*—topographical lore. Yet it is fun to be your own placename translator. Included in this book is a useful list of common Irish placename elements. They are given first in their Gaelic form, then in the various forms one may meet in actual placenames and finally a translation of the Gaelic element. For example, *baile* which is often found as "bally" or "bal" means "town" or "townland," *caiseal* which appears as "cashel" means "circular stone fort" and since colour played a large part in the imagination of the original of the old namers, *buí* which means "yellow" occurs in such places as Mullaghboy.

The beginner should try to discover the name in Gaelic first. This obviates much difficulty. Let us take the places names Annascaul, Annacloy and Annaghaskin. The "Anna"s are all the same, yet the Gaelic forms of the names of these places are *Abhainn an Scáil* (the river of the hero), *Áth na Cloiche* (the ford of the stone) and *Éanach na nEascoinn* (the marsh of the eels) "Tis a puzzlement," as the King of Siam said to another Anna. Yet it is not only great fun but a continuing intellectual pleasure to recognise and know the meaning of a *dún*, a *carraig*, a *droim*, a *tulach*, a *lios* and a *ráth*. Ireland is full of this buried treasure. And as for the name given by the joker to Tandgragee and by the poet to Glenagivney, well you are just going to have to look them up!

Note:
Where the place has been given a (later) English name this is
indicated in the list by (Eng.) appearing after this name. The
older Irish name is then given. Where the Irish name is hard
to translate, as it frequently is, and uses form of words not
known to modern Irish the mark (obs.) = "obscure" is given
before a possible meaning Sometimes detailed local know-
ledge is essential; sometimes it is inaccurate and misleading.
Finally many dead personalities like the Brian of *Translations* have left their mark and their names in places to confuse
us further. It is a continuing and maddening study.

DIY Dinnseanchas

The placenames given in this book, those of the cities, the towns and larger villages, are the merest fraction of the number that exists. From the window of the room where I am writing this I can see, without much craning of the neck, Shantallow, Culmore, Coolkeeragh, Edenballymore, Altnagelvin, Benevenagh, Benone, Gobnascale, Templemore, Clondermot and Corrody. Even those are only a selection: every parish, every townland, practically every field has it own name. It would be almost impossible to list them all. Yet each interested person can become quite an efficient construer of placenames. This list of commonly occurring elements will be a great help. Try to discover the name in Irish; signposts will help and many modern maps give Irish versions as well as English. From this form of the name easily identifiable elements can be picked out. In our list the Irish root-word is given first, then the modified form in which it may appear in the modern name and finally the meaning of the Irish root. So after some practice, the list I gave above as being on view from my window will hold no terrors for the assiduous "Dinnseanchas"-er!

Abha (a, aw, ou, ow,owen): river
Achadh (a, agh, agha, augh, aughey): field
Áltt (alt): ravine, deep valley
Árd (ar, ard): high, height
Áth (a, ah, aha, ath): ford

Baile (bal, bally, vally, ville): town, steading, townland
Bán (bane, baun, bawn): white
Barr (Bar, barr, baur): top
Beag (beg): small
Béal (ball, bell): mouth
Bealach (bal, ballagh, vally): way, pass, highroad
Beann (ben, bin, pin): peak, mountain
Bearna (s)(barn, barna, barnes, varna): gap
Beith (Beagh, behy, beha,vehy): beech tree
Bó (bo, boe, mo, moe): cow
Bóthar (Boher, booter, batter, voher): road
Brú (bru, bruff): hostel,palace
Buí (boy, bwee): yellow
Bun (bon, bun): base, foot

Caiseal (cashel, castle, goshel): stone fort
Caisleán (cashlaun): castle
Caoin (kean, keen): pleasant, gentle
Caol (keel, kil, kill): narrow
Carn (carn, carna): heap
Carraig (carrick, carrig): rock
Cathair (caher, cahir); fort
Ceann (*Cionn*) (kan, ken, can): head
Ceapach (cappa, cappagh, cappo): plot of land
Ceathrú (carrow, carhoo): quarter (land-measure)

Ceis (kesh, kish): wickerwork, causeway
Cill (kil, kill,): church, cell
Clann (clan): family, tribe
Cloch (clogh, clough): stone
Clochán (cloghan, cloghane, clifden): stepping-stones
Clochar (clogher): stone building, stony place
Cluain (clon, cloon, cloone): meadow
Cnoc (crock, knock): hill
Coill (kil, kyle, kill): wood
Cora (cor, corra, curra): weir
Corr (cor, corr, curr): hill
Cos (cosh, cush, cuss): foot, mouth of a river
Cruach (crogh, croagh): rick, hill
Cúil (col, cool, cul): recess, corner
Currach (curra, curragh, curry): marsh

Daingean (dangan, dingle): stronghold
Dearg (derg): red
Díseart (desart, disert, dysert): hermitage
Doire (darry, derry, der): oak tree, oak grove
Domhnach (donagh, donough, dun): large (Patrician)church
Droichead (drait, drehid, drohed, tred): bridge
Dro (i)*m* (drom, drum, drim): ridge
Dubh (doo, duff, duv): black

Each (augh, ach, eigh): steed
Éadan (eden): hill-brow
Eaglais (aglish, eglis, eglish): church
Eanach (anna, annagh, enny): marshy ground
Eas (ass, assy, ess): waterfall, cascade
Eó (o, oe, yo): yew tree

Faithche (faha, fahy, feigh): green
Fál (fal, falls): hedge, enclosure
Fearn (farn, farnagh): alder tree
Fia (eigh, eag, ee): deer
Fiodh (fee, feigh, fi): wood
Fionn (fin, finn, inn): white, fair
Fraoch (freagh, free): heather

Gabhal (gole, goole, goul): fork
Gall (gal, gall, gaul): foreigner
Gaoth (gwee): inlet
Garbh (garra, garriff, garve): rough
Garraí (gar, garry): garden
Geal (gal,gil): white, bright
Glas (glas, glass): grey, green
Gleann (glan, glen, glyn): valley
Gort (gort, gurt): field
Grian (green, gren, greany): sun
Grianán (greenan): summer-house

Inis (inch, innis, ennis, nish): island, holm
Inbhear (inver, enner, ineer): river-mouth
Iúr (ure): yew tree

Lag (lag, lig, lug): hollow, pool
Lann (lan, lann): church
Leaba (labba, labby): bed
Leac (lack, leck, leek, lick): flagstone
Leath (la, lah, le): half
Leathan (lahan, lane): wide, broad
Léim (leam, lem, lim): leap

Leitir (letter, lettera, leteragh): (wet)hillside
Lios (lis, liss): enclosure, ringfort
Loch (lough, low): lake, sea-inlet
Long (long): ship

Machaire (maghera, maghery): plain
Magh (ma, may, moy, maw, muff): plain
Mainistir (monaster): abbey
Maol (meel. moyle): smooth, bald
Mín (min, meen): smooth, level ground
Móin (mona, mone): peat bog
Mór (more): big, great
Muc (muck): pig
Muileann (mullen, mullin): mill
Muine (money): thicket
Mullach (mullagh): summit, crown

Nead (nad): nest
Nua (noo, nou, noe): new

Óg (oge, og, ock): young, small
Oileán (illan): island

Poll (poll, poul): hole
Port (port, fort): harbour, fort

Ráth (ra, rath, raha): ringfort
Reilig (rellig): graveyard
Rua (roe, rua): red-haired, russet

Sagart (saggart, taggart): priest

Saileach (sillagh, sallagh, sill): willow, sally
Sean (shan): old
Sí (shee): fairy (mound)
Sionnach (shinny, tinny): fox
Sliabh (sle, slew, slieve): mountain
Slua (sloe): host
Sráid (sraud, straid, strad): street
Suí (see, se, sea, shi): seat

Tearmann (termon): sanctuary land
Teach, *Tigh* (ta, sta, ti, sti, taugh): house, monastery
Teampall (tample, temple): church
Tír (tir, tyr): country, territory
Tobar (tober, tobber, tubber): well
Tóchar (togher): causeway
Tiobra (i)d (tibber, tibret, tipper, tubbrid): well
Tuaim (tom, toom, tum, tuam): tomb, grave-mound
Trá (tra, tragh, traw, tray): strand
Tuar (tore, toor, tour): milking-place, bleach-green
Tulach (tul, tulagh, tullow, tully): small hill

Uisce (isk, iska, isky): water
Uaimhe (hoe): cave

Connacht—*Cúige Chonnacht*

County Galway—*Contae na Gaillimhe*

Ahascragh	Áth Eascrach	Ford of the esker
Ardrahan	Ard Raithin	Height of the ferns
Athenry	Baile Átha an Rí	The town of the ford of the king
Aughrim	Eachroim	Steed ridge
Ballinafad	Béal an Átha Fada	Mouth of the long ford
Ballinasloe	Béal Átha na Sluaighe	Fordmouth of the hosts
Ballindereen	Baile an Doirín	Town of the little oakgrove
Ballyconneely	Baile Conaola	Conaola's townland
Ballyconree	Baile Conraoi	Conraoi's townland
Ballycrissane	Baile Crosáin	Crossan's townland
Ballygar	Béal Átha Ghártha	Fordmouth of the garden
Ballyglunin	Béal Átha Glúinín	Gluinin's fordmouth
Ballymacward	Baile Mhic an Bhaird	Town of the poet's son
Ballymoe	Baile Átha Mó	Mo's fordmouth
Ballynahown	Baile na hAbhann	River town
Ballyshrule	Baile Sruthail	Town of the stream
Barna	Bearna	Gap
Barnaderg	Bearna Dhearg	Red gap
Bealadangan	Béal an Daingin	The fortress entrance
Belclare	Béal Chláir	Mouth of the plain
Bohermore	An Bóthar Mór	The high road
Boyounagh	Buíbheanach	Yellow marsh
Caherlistrane	Cathair Loistreáin	Stone fort of burnt corn
Caltra	An Chealtrach	The burial place
Camus	Camas	River (or road) bend

Cappataggle	Ceapaigh an tSeagail	The rye-plot
Carna	Carna	(obs.) Flesh?
Carraroe	An Cheathrú Rua	The russet-coloured quarter
Cashel	An Caiseal	The stone fort
Claddaghduff	An Cladach Dubh	The black strand
Claregalway (Eng.)	Baile Chláir	The town of the plain
Clarinbridge	Droichead an Chláirín	Bridge of the little plain
Cleggan	An Cloigeann	The skull
Clifden	An Clochán	The stepping-stones
Cloghbrack	An Chloch Bhreac	Speckled stone
Clonbern	Cluain Bheirn	Bearn's meadow
Clonfert	Cluain Fearta	Meadow of the grave
Clontuskert	Cluain Tuaiscirt	North meadow
Cloonminda	Cluain Mionda	Small meadow
Collinamuck	Caladh na Muc	Landing-place of the swine
Cornamona	Corr na Móna	The bog-spit
Corrandulla	Cor an Dola	Twist of the cable
Costelloe	Casla	Sea-inlet
Craughwell	Creachmhaoil	Plunder store
Creggs	Na Creaga	The rocks
Cummer	Comar	Channel
Currandrum	Cor an Droma	The twisted ridge
Derreen	Doirín	The little oakgrove
Derrybrien	Daraidh Braoin	Braon's oakgrove
Dunmore	Dún Mór	Great fort
Errislannan	Iorras Fhlannáin	Flannan's height
Galway	Gaillimh	(Place) of Gailleamh
Glenamaddy	Gleann na Madadh	The glen of the dogs
Gort	An Gort	The tilled field
Gurteen	Goirtín	Little field
Gurteeny	Goirtíní	Little fields
Gurtymadden	Gort Uí Mhadaín	Madden's field
Inishbofin	Inis Bó Finne	The island of the white cow

Connacht—*Cúige Chonnacht*

Inishere	Inis Oírr	East island
Inishmaan	Inis Meáin	Middle island
Kilcolgan	Cill Cholgáin	Church of St Colga
Kilconly	Cill Chonla	Church of St Conla
Kilconnell	Cill Chonaill	Church of St Conall
Kilchreest	Cill Chríost	Christchurch
Kilkerrin	Cill Chiaráin	Church of St Ciaran
Killeenadeema	Cillín a Díoma	Little church of St Dioma
Killimor	Cill Iomair	Church of St Iomar
Killoran	Cill Odhráin	Church of St Oran
Kilmurvey	Cill Mhuirbhigh	Church of the seashore
Kilrickle	Cill Rícill	Church of St Riceall
Kilronan	Cill Rónáin	Church of St Ronan
Kilsallagh	Coill Salach	Willow wood
Kinvara	Cinn Mhara	Sea headlands
Kylebrack	An Choill Bhreac	The speckled wood
Kylemore	An Choill Mhóir	The great wood
Leenane	An Líonán	Tide-fill
Letterfrack	Leitir Fraic	Frack's hillside
Lettermore	Leitir Móir	Mor's hillside
Lettermullen	Leitir Mealláin	Meallan's hillside
Levally	An Leathbhaile	Half-townland
Loughrea	Baile Locha Riach	Town of the grey lake
Maam	An Mám	High pass
Menlough	Mionlach	Smooth pasture
Monivea	Muine Mheá	Mea's thicket
Moyard	Maigh Ard	High plain
Moycullen	Maigh Cuilinn	Holly plain
Moyglass	Maigh Ghlas	Green plain
Moylough	Maigh Locha	Lake plain
Oranmore	Órán Mór	Great cold spring
Oughterard	Uachtar Ard	Upper height
Ower	Odhar	Dark (place)

Portumna	Port Omna	Port of the tree-trunk
Renvyle	Rinn Mhaoile	Bare headland
Rosmuck	Ros Muc	Headland of pigs
Rosscahill	Ros Cathail	Charles's headland
Rossmore	Ros Mór	Great headland
Spiddal	An Spidéal	The hospital
Toomard	Tuaim Ard	High burial mound
Tuam	Tuaim	Grave mound
Tubber	An Tobar	The well
Turloughmore	An Turlach Mór	Large disappearing lake

County Leitrim—*Contae Liatroma*

Aghacashel	Achadh an Chaisil	Castle field
Aghavas	Achadh an Mheasa	Mast field
Annaghmore	Eanach Mór	Big marsh
Aughamore	Achadh Mór	Big field
Ballinaglera	Baile na gCléireach	Clerks town
Bornacoola	Barr na Cúile	The head of the corner
Carrigallen	Carraig álainn	Beautiful rock
Cloone	An Chluain	The meadow
Cooligrain	Cúl le Gréin	Sunny corner
Corrawallan	Corr an Mhailín	The hollow of the purse
Corriga	Carraigigh	Rocky place
Derradda	Doire Fhada	Long oakgrove
Dromahair	Droim Dhá Eithiar	Ridge of two demons
Dromod	Dromad	Ridge
Drumcong	Droim Conga	Ridge of the isthmus
Drumkeerin	Droim Caorthainn	Rowan tree ridge
Drumshambo	Droim Seanbhó	Old cow ridge
Drumsna	Droim ar Snámh	Ridge over the swimming place
Garadice	Garbhros	Rough peninsula
Glenade	Gleann Éada	Eada's valley
Glenboy	Gleann Buí	Yellow glen
Glencar	Gleann an Chairthe	Glen of the standing stone
Glenfarne	Gleann Fearna	Alder glen
Gorvagh	Garbhach	Rough place
Gurteen	Goirtín	Little field

Keshcarrigan	Ceis Chairrigín	Wicker causeway of the little rock
Kilbracken	Coill Bhreacán	Bramble wood
Kilclare	Coill an Chláir	The wood of the plain
Killargue	Cill Fhearga	Church of St Fearga
Killegar	Coill an Ghairr	Pulp wood
Kilnagross	Coill na gCros	The wood of the crosses
Kiltyclogher	Coillte Clochair	Woods of the stony place
Kinlough	Cionn Locha	Lake head
Largydonnell	Learga Uí Dhónaill	O'Donnell's slope
Leckaun	An Leacán	The disc-stone
Leitrim	Liatroim	Grey ridge
Lissinagroagh	Lisín na gCruach	Rick enclosure
Mohill	Maothail	Soft land
Rossinver	Ros Inbhir	Estuary headland
Tarmon	An Tearmann	The sanctuary land
Tullaghan	An Tulachán	The little hill
Tullycooley	Tulaigh an Chuaille	The hillock of the stake

County Mayo—*Contae Mhaigh Eo*

Aghagower	Achadh Ghobhair	Field of the well
Aghamore	Achadh Mór	Big field
Ardnaree	Ard na Ria	Height of the executions
Attymachugh	Áit Tí Mhic Aodha	House site of the son of Hugh
Ayle	An Aill	The cliff
Balla	Balla	Well
Ballina	Béal an Átha	The mouth of the ford
Ballindine	Baile an Daighin	The town of the fortress
Ballinrobe	Baile an Roba	The town of the (river) Robe
Ballintubber	Baile an Tobair	The town of the well
Ballycroy	Baile Chruaich	The town of the peak
Ballyfarna	Bealach Fearna	Alderway
Ballyglass	An Baile Glas	The grey town
Ballyhaunis	Béal Átha hAmhnais	The mouth of the severe ford
Ballyhean	Béal Átha héin	Fordmouth of the bird
Ballysakeery	Baile Easa Caoire	Town of the waterfall of the berry
Bangor Erris	Baingear	(obs.) Pointed hills?
Barnatra	Barr na Trá	The top of the strand
Barnycarroll	Bearna Chearúill	Carroll's gap
Bekan Cross	Béacán	Sprout
Belcarra	Baile na Cora	The town of the twists
Belderrig	Béal Deirg	Dearg's estuary
Bellacorick	Béal Átha Chomhraic	Ford mouth of the confluence
Belmullet	Béal an Mhuirthead	Entrance to the Mullet peninsula
Bofeenaun	Both Faonáin	Fionan's hut

Bohola	Both Chomhla	Comhla's hut
Bonniconlon	Muine Chonalláin	Conlon's thicket
Boughadoon	Both an Dúin	Hut of the fort
Breaghwy	Bréachmhaigh	Beautiful plain
Brickens	Na Broicíní	The badger warrens
Bunnacurry	Bun an Churraigh	The entrance to the marsh
Bunnahowen	Bun na hAbhna	Mouth of the river
Callow	An Caladh	The landing place
Carrowbeg	An Cheathrú Bheag	The little quarter
Carrowholly	Ceathrú Chalaidh	The landing-place quarter
Carrownisky	Ceathrú an Uisce	The water quarter
Carrowteige	Ceathrú Thaidhg	Tadhg's quarter
Castlebar	Caisleán an Bharraigh	Barry's castle
Claremorris	Clár Chlainne Mhuiris	Plain of the family of Muiris
Cloghbrack	An Chloch Bhreac	The speckled stone
Clogher	An Clochar	Stony place
Cloghmore	An Chloich Mhóir	(Place of) the big stone
Cloondaff	Cluain Damh	Church meadow
Cloonfallagh	Cluain Falach	Fenced meadow
Cloontia	Na Cluainte	The meadows
Cong	Conga	Isthmus
Corroy	Corr Ráithe	The projection of the rath
Cregganbaun	An Creagán Bán	White rocky place
Crossmolina	Crois Mhaoilíona	Maoilíona's cross
Cuilmore	An Choill Mhór	The big wood
Culleens	Na Coillíní	The little woods
Currane	An Corrán	The sickle-shaped place
Derryvohy	Doire Bhoithe	The oak-grove of the hut
Dooagh	Dumha Acha	Sandbank
Doocastle	Caisleán an Dumha	Mound castle
Doohoma	Dumha Thuama	Grave cairn
Dooleeg	Dumha Liag	Headstone cairn
Drummin	An Dromainn	The ridge

Connacht—*Cúige Chonnacht*

Dugort	Dumha Goirt	Field-cairn
Garranard	Garrán Ard	High grove
Geesala	Gaoth Sáile	Salt water inlet
Glenamoy	Gleann na Muaidhe	Valley of the (river) Moy
Inishbiggle	Inis Bigil	Island of fasting
Inishturk	Inis Toirc	Boar island
Islandeady	Oileán Eadaí	Clothes island
Keel	An Caol	The isthmus
Keenaghbeg	Caonach Beag	Little mossy place
Kilkelly	Cill Cheallaigh	Ceallach's church
Killadoon	Coill an Dúin	Fortwood
Killala	Cill Ala	Ala's church
Killasser	Cill Lasrach	Fiery church (or Lasair's church)
Killateeaun	Coill an tSiáin	The wood of the fairy mound
Killavally	Coill an Bhaile	The wood of the town
Killour	Coill Odhar	Dark wood
Kilmaine	Cill Mheáin	Middle church
Kilmovee	Cill Moibhí	St Mobhi's church
Kilsallagh	Coill Salach	Willow wood
Kiltimagh	Coillte Mach	Woods of the plain
Kincun	Cionn Con	Hound's head
Knock	An Cnoc	The hill
Knockanillaun	Cnoc an Oileáin	Hill of the island
Knockmore	An Cnoc Mór	The big hill
Lahardane	Leathardán	Sloping terrace
Liscarney	Lios Cearnaigh	Cearnach's ringfort
Lissatava	Lios an tSamhaidh	Ringfort of the sorrel
Lurga	An Lorgain	The strip of land
Manulla	Maigh Nulla	Nulla's plain
Mayo	Maigh Eo	Plain of the yew trees
Mulrany	An Mhala Raithní	The ferny hill-brow
Murneen	Muirnín	Sweetheart
Murrisk	Muraisc	Sea-marsh

Neale	An Éill	(obs.) Nestling?
Orlar	Urlár	Floor
Park	An Pháirc	The field
Pulathomas	Poll an Tómais	The hole of homage
Raheens	Na Ráithíní	The little forts
Rathnamagh	Ráth na Mach	The ringfort of the plain
Roonah	Rú an Átha	Rue (growing) at the ford
Scardaune	Scardán	Water jet
Sheean	An Sián	Fairy mound
Shraheens	Na Sraithíní	Little swathes
Shrule	Sruthair	Stream
Srah	An tSraith	The swathe
Srahmore	An Srath Mór	The large holm
Straid	An tSráid	The street
Tagheen	Teách Chaoin	Caon's house
Tonragee	Tóin re Gaoth	Leeward (lit. arse to wind)
Tooreen	An Tuairín	Little bleach-green
Tourmakeady	Tuar Mhic Éadaigh	Keady's bleach-green
Tulrahan	Tulach Shrutháin	Hillock of the stream
Turlough	Turlach	Dry lake
Ummoon	Iomún	Trout

County Roscommon—*Contae Ros Comáin*

Arigna	An Airgnigh	Destroyer (name of a river)
Athleague	Áth Liag	Ford of the standing stones
Ballaghaderreen	Bealach an Doirín	The road of the little oakgrove
Ballanagare	Béal Átha na gCarr	Fordmouth of the cars
Ballinameen	Béal an Átha Mín	Mouth of the smooth ford
Ballinlough	Baile an Locha	The town of the lake
Ballintubber	Baile an Tobair	The town of the well
Ballydangan	Baile Daighean	Fortified town
Ballyfarnon	Béal Átha Fearnáin	Fearnan's fordmouth
Ballyforan	Béal Átha Feorainne	Fordmouth of the holm
Ballymacurley	Baile Mhic Thorlaigh	Torlough's town
Baylough	Béal Lathaí	Liquor mouth
Bealnamulla	Béal Átha na Muille	Fordmouth of the mule
Boyle	Mainistir na Búille	Monastery of the (river) Boyle
Callow	An Caladh	The landing-place
Carracastle	Ceathrú an Chaisil	Quarter of the stone fort
Carrowbehy	Ceathrú Bheithí	Birch-quarter
Castlerea	An Caisleán Riabhach	The grey castle
Cloonfad	Cluain Fada	Longmeadow
Cloonyquin	Cluain Uí Choinn	Quinn's meadow
Cornafulla	Corr na Fola	Bloody projection
Corrigeenroe	Carraigín Rua	Little red rock
Croghan	Cruachán	Peak
Curraghboy	An Currach Buí	The yellow marsh
Curraghroe	An Currach Rua	The red marsh

Derreenargan	Doirín Argan	The little oakgrove of the plunder
Donamon	Dún Iomáin	Ioman's fort
Drummullin	Droim an Mhuilinn	Millridge
Dysart	An Díseart	The hermitage
Elphin	Ail Finn	Rock of the clear spring
Garranlahan	An Garrán Leathan	The broad grove
Keadue	Céideadh	Flat-topped hill
Kilglass	Cill Ghlais	Grey church
Kilmore	Cill Mhór	Big church
Kllrooskey	Coill na Rúscaí	Wood of the rustling
Kilteevan	Cill Taobháin	Taobhan's church
Kiltoom	Cill Tuama	Church of the burial mound
Knockcroghery	Cnoc an Chrochaire	Hangman's hill
Knockvicar	Cnoc an Bhiocáire	Vicar's hill
Lackin	An Leacain	Flagstone
Lecarrow	An Leithcheathrú	The half-quarter
Lisacul	Lios an Choill	Woodfort
Lissalway	Lios Sealbhaigh	Fort of the herd
Lurgan	An Lorgain	The strip of land
Mantua	An Móinteach	The moss
Moyne	An Mhaighean	The precinct
Rahara	Ráth Ara	The ringfort of the charioteer
Rinn a Rodáin	Roinn an Rodáin	The tract of the path
Roscommon	Ros Comáin	St Coman's wood
Ruskey	Rúscaigh	Marshy place
Taughmaconnell	Teach Mhic Conaill	Conall's son's house
Tibohine	Tigh Baoithín	St Baoithin's house
Trien	An Trian	Thirding

County Sligo—*Contae Sligigh*

Achonry	Achadh Conaire	Conaire's field
Aclare	Áth an Chláir	The ford of the plank
Ballinacarrow	Baile na Cora	The town of the twists
Ballinafad	Béal an Átha Fada	The mouth of the long ford
Ballindoon	Baile an Dúin	The town of the fort
Ballinfull	Baile an Phoill	The town of the hole
Baillintogher	Baile an Tóchair	The town of the causeway
Ballintrillick	Béal Átha an Trí Liag	The mouth of the ford of the three headstones
Ballisodare	Baile Easa Dara	Town of the waterfall of the oak
Ballygawley	Baile Uí Dhalaigh	Daly's town
Ballymote	Baile an Mhóta	Town of the mound
Beltra	Béal Trá	Mouth of the strand
Bunnanadden	Bun an Fheadáin	Foot of the gulley
Carrowneadan	Ceathrú an Éadain	Front quarter
Castlegal	Caisle Geala	Bright stone forts
Castlegarren	Caiseal an Ghearráin	Stone fort of the gelding
Cliffoney	Cliafuine	Hurdle thicket
Cloghboley	Clochbhuaile	Stone circle
Cloonacool	Cluain na Cúile	Rear meadow
Cloonkeavy	Cluain Ciabhaigh	Ciabhach's meadow
Cloonloo	Cluain Lua	Lua's meadow
Colgagh	Calgach	Prickly place
Collooney	Cúil Mhuine	Recess of the thicket
Coolaney	Cúil Áine	Anne's recess

Corballa	An Corrbhaile	The odd town
Culfadda	Coill Fhada	Long wood
Curry	An Choraidh	The weir
Dromard	An Droim Ard	High ridge
Drumcliffe	Droim Chliabh	Ridge of baskets
Drumfin	Droim Fionn	Fair ridge
Easky	Iascaigh	Abounding in fish
Gleneask	Gleann Iasc	Fish glen
Grange	An Ghráinseach	Granary
Gurteen	Goirtín	Little field
Inniscrone	Inis Crabhann	Holm of the river-esker
Keash	An Chéis	Wattled causeway
Kilfree	Cill Fraoigh	Heather church
Kilglass	Cill Ghlas	Grey church
Killavil	Cill Fhábhail	St Fabhal's church
Kilmactranny	Cill Mhic Treana	Mac Trean's church
Knocknahur	Cnoc na hIora	Squirrel hill
Lavagh	Leamhach	Marshmallow
Lisserlough	Liosar Locha	Ringfort by the lough
Monasteraden	Mainistir Réadáin	(obs.) Monastery of the star?
Moneygold	Muine Dhúltaigh	Dualta's thicket
Mullaghmore	An Mullach Mór	The large hilltop
Owenbeg	An Abhainn Bheag	The little river
Rathlee	Ráth Lao	Ringfort of the calves
Rathmullen	Ráth an Mhuillinn	The ringfort of the mill
Rosses Point (Eng.)	An Ros	The promontory
Skreen	An Scrín	The shrine
Sligo	Sligeach	Shelly place
Strandhill (Eng.)	An Leathros	Sandy spit
Templeboy	Teampall Baoith	Baoth's church
Tourlestrane	Tuar Loistreáin	Loistrean's bleachgreen
Tubbercurry	Tobar an Choire	The well of the cauldron

Leinster—*Cúige Laighean*

County Carlow—*Contae Cheatharlach*

Ardattin	Ard Aitinn	Aiteann's height
Bennekerry	Binn an Choire	The peak of the cauldron
Borris	An Bhuiríos	Borough
Carlow	Ceatharlach	(obs.) Quadruple lake?
Clonegal	Cluain na nGall	The meadow of the foreigners
Clonmore	Cluain Mhór	Large meadow
Corries Cross	Crois na gCoraí	Wrestlers cross
Fenagh	Fionnmhac	Fair son
Garryhill	An Gharbhchoill	The rough wood
Graiguecullen	An Ghráig	Village (of the holly?)
Kilbride	Cill Bhríde	St Brigid's Church
Kildavin	Cill Damháin	Damhan's church
Killerig	Cill Dheirge	St Deirg's church
Leighlinnbridge	Leithghlinn an Droichid	Small glen of the bridge
Muine Bheag	Muine Bheag	Small thicket
Myshall	Míseal	(obs.) Misdirection?
Nurney	An Urnaí	The oratory
Rathtoe	Ráth Tó	To's ringfort
Rathvilly	Ráth Bhile	Ringfort of the tree
Tullow	An Tulach	The hillock

County Dublin—*Contae Bhaile Átha Cliath*

Artane	Ard Aidhin	Aidhean's height
Balbriggan	Baile Brigín	Brigin's town
Baldoyle	Baile Dúill	Dougal's town
Ballsbridge (Eng.)	Droichead na Dothra	Dodder bridge
Ballyboden	Baile Baodáin	Baodan's town
Ballyboughal	Baile Bachaille	Crozier town
Ballybrack	An Baile Breac	Speckled town
Ballyfermot	Baile Formaid	Formad's town
Booterstown	Baile an Bhóthair	Road town
Brittas	An Briotás	The brattice
Cabinteely	Cábán tSíle	Sheila's cottage
Cabra	An Chabrach	The poor land
Cappagh	Ceapach	Plot of land
Carrickmines	Carraig Mhaighin	Rock of the steading
Castleknock	Caisleán Cnucha	Castle of the mound
Chapelizod	Séipéal Iosóid	Isolde's chapel
Cloghran	Clochrán	Stepping-stones
Clondalkin	Cluain Dolcáin	Dolcan's meadow
Clonsilla	Cluain Saileach	Osier meadow
Coolock	An Chúlóg	Recess
Crumlin	Cromghlinn	Crooked glen
Dalkey (Scand.)	Deilginis	Thorn island
Dolphin's Barn (Eng.)	Carnán	Cairn
Donabate	Domhnach Bat	(obs.) Church of the boat?
Donnybrook	Domhnach Broc	(obs.) Broc's church?

Leinster—*Cúige Laighean*

Donnycarney	Domhnach Cearna	Cearna's church
Drimnagh	Droimeanach	Place of ridges
Drumcondra	Droim Conrach	(obs.) Conrach's ridge?
Drummartin	Droim Máirtín	Martin's ridge
Dublin	Baile Átha Cliath	Hurdlefordtown
Dundrum	Dún Droma	Fort of the ridge
Dún Laoghaire	Dún Laoire	Laoire's fort
Finglas	Fionnghlas	Clear stream
Glasthule	Glas Tuathail	Tuathal's streamlet
Howth (Eng.)	Beann Éadair	Eadar's peak
Inchicore	Inse Chór	(obs.)Twisted holm?
Kilbarrack	Cill Bharróg	Barrog's church
Killester	Cill Easra	Easra's church
Killiney	Cill Iníon Léinín	Church of the daughters of Leinin
Kilmainham	Cill Mhaighneann	Maighne's church
Kilsallaghan	Cill Shalcháin	Salchan's church
Kilternan	Cill Tiarnáin	Tiarnan's church
Lucan	Leamchán	Place of the mallows
Lusk	Lusca	Cave
Malahide	Mullach Íde	Ide's hilltop
Merrion	Muirfin	Seashore
Mulhuddart	Mullach Eadrad	Eadrad's hilltop
Naul	An Aill	The cliff
Portmarnock	Port Mearnóg	St Mearnog's harbour
Raheny	Ráth Eanaigh	Eanna's ringfort
Ranelagh (Scand.)	Raghnallach	Raghnall's land
Rathcoole	Ráth Cúil	Cul's ringfort
Rathfarnham	Ráth Fearnáin	Fearnan's ringfort
Rathgar	Ráth Garbh	Rough ringfort
Rathmines	Ráth Maonais	Maonas's ringfort
Ring Commons	Coimín na Roinne	Commonland of the share
Ringsend	An Rinn	The headland
Rush	An Ros	The headland

Saggart	Teach Sagard	St Sagard's house
Sallynoggin	An Naigín	The noggin
Santry	Seantrabh	Old tribe
Shankill	Seanchill	Old church
Skerries	Na Sceirí	Sea rocks
Stillorgan	Stigh Lorgan	Lorcan's House
Sutton (Eng.)	Cill Fhionntain	St Fintan's Church
Swords	Sord	Sward
Tallaght	Tamhlacht	Grave
Templeogue	Teach Mealóg	Mealóg's house
Terenure	Tír an Iúir	The land of yew
Windy Arbour (Eng.)	Na Glasáin	The finches

County Kildare—*Contae Chill Dara*

Athgarvan	Áth Garbháin	Garbhan's ford
Athy	Baile Átha Í	The town of Ae's ford
Ballymore	An Baile Mór	Big town
Ballytore	Béal Átha an Tuair	The fordmouth of the bleach-green
Brannockstown	Baile na mBreatnach	Welshtown
Cadamstown	Baile Mhic Ádaim	Macadam's town
Calverstown	Baile an Chalbhaigh	Town of the bald man
Carbury	Cairbre	(obs.) Rocky place?
Carragh	Ceárach	(obs.) Rocky terrain?
Castledermot (Eng.)	Díseart Diarmada	St Dermot's hermitage
Celbridge	Cill Droichid	Bridge church
Clane	Claonadh	Slope
Clongowes Wood	Coill Chluana Gabhann	Wood of the smith's meadow
Coolcarrigan	Cúil Charraigín	The rocky recess
Donadea	Domhnach Dheá	Dea's church
Kilberry	Cill Bhearaigh	St Bearach's church
Kilcock	Cill Choca	St Coca's church
Kilcullen	Cill Chuillinn	Cuillean's church
Kildangan	Cill Daingin	Church of the fortification
Kildare	Cill Dara	Church of the oak
Kill	An Chill	The church
Kilmead	Cill Míde	St Míde's church
Kilmeague	Cill Maodhóg	St Maodhóg's church
Leixlip (Eng.)	Léim an Bhradáin	Salmon leap

Maynooth	Maigh Nuad	Nua's plain
Monasterevan	Mainistir Eimhín	St Eimhin's monastery
Moone	Maoin	Property
Moyvalley	Maigh Bhealaigh	Plain of the road
Naas	An Nás	The fair
Narraghmore	An Fhorrach Mhór	The great tract of land
Nurney	An Urnaí	The oratory
Prosperous (Eng.)	An Chorrchoill	The odd or misplaced wood
Rathangan	Ráth Iomgháin	Iomghan's ringfort
Rathmore	An Ráth Mhór	The large ringfort
Sallins	Na Solláin	(obs.) The willow groves?
Straffan	Teach Srafáin	Srafan's church

County Kilkenny—*Contae Chill Chainnigh*

Ballyfoyle	Baile an Phoill	The town of the hole
Ballyhale	Baile Héil	Haol's town
Ballyragget	Béal Átha Ragad	Fordmouth of Ragad
Callan	Callainn	(obs.) Clamour?
Castlecomer	Caisleán an Chomair	The castle of the confluence
Clifden (Eng.)	Ráth Gharbháin	Garbhan's ring-fort
Clogh	An Chloch	The stone
Coolbawn	An Cúl Bán	The white recess
Coolcullen	Cúl an Chuillin	Holly recess
Coon	An Cuan	The harbour
Danesfort	Dún Feart	The fort of the miracle
Dungarvan	Dún Garbháin	Garbhan's fort
Dunnamaggan	Dún Iomagáin	Iomagan's fort
Fiddown	Fiodh Dúin	Fort of the forest
Galmoy	Gabhalmhaigh	Plain of the fork
Gathabawn	An Geata Bán	The white gate
Glenmore	An Gleann Mór	The great glen
Goresbridge (Eng.)	An Droichead Nua	The new bridge
Graiguenamanagh	Gráig na Managh	The village of the monks
Inistioge	Inis Tíog	Tiog's holm
Kells	Ceanannas	Headquarters
Kilkenny	Cill Chainnigh	St Canice's church
Kilmacow	Cill Mhic Bhúith	St Mochua's church
Kilmanagh	Cill Mhanach	Monk's church
Kilmoganny	Cill Mogeanna	St Mogeanna's Church

Knocktopher	Cnoc an Tóchair	The hill of the causeway
Mooncoin	Móin Choinn	Bog of the hound
Mullinavat	Muileann an Bhata	The mill of the stick
Owning	Ónainn	(obs.) Stony place?
Piltown	Baile an Phoill	Town of the hole
Rathmoyle	An Ráth Mhaol	The smooth ringfort
Skeaghvasteen	Sceach an Mhaistín	The hawthorn of the mastiff
Slieverue	Sliabh Rua	Red mountain
Stoneyford	Áth an Staing	The ford of the stang
Templeorum	Teampall Fhothram	Church of the tumult
Thomastown (Eng.)	Baile Mhic Andái	Fitzanthony's town
Three Castles (Eng.)	Babhún Ón Duach	(obs.) Jove's bailey?
Tullaroan	Tulach Ruáin	The hilltop of the red-haired person
Tullogher	Tulachar	(obs.) Hilly place?
Urlingford	Áth na nUrlainn	The ford of the forecourts
Woodsgift	Baile na Lochán	The town of the pool

County Laois—*Contae Laoise*

Abbeyleix	Mainistir Laoise	The monastery of Laois
Aghavoe	Achadh Bhó	Field of the cow
Attanna	Áth Tanaí	Narrow ford
Ballacolla	Baile Cholla	Body town
Ballickmoyler	Baile Mhic Mhaoilir	MacMaoilir's town
Ballinakill	Baile na Coille	Town of the wood
Balloughmore	An Bealach Mór	The high road
Ballybrittas	Baile Briotáis	Town of the brattice
Ballybrophy	Baile Uí Bhróithe	Brophy's town
Ballyfin	An Baile Fionn	The bright town
Ballylinan	Baile Uí Laigheanáin	Lynan's town
Ballyroan	Baile Átha an Róine	Town of the ford of the hair
Borris-in-Ossory	Buiríos Mór Osraí	Big borough of Ossory
Camross	Camros	Twisted promontory
Clonaslee	Cluain na Slí	The meadow of the road
Clough	An Chloch	The stone
Coolrain	Cúil Ruáin	Red-haired person's recess
Crettyard	Crochta Ard	High croft
Cullahill	An Chúlchoill	The black wood
Donaghmore	Domhnach Mór	Big church
Durrow	Darú	Oakfield
Emo	Ioma	Bed
Kilbricken	Cill Bhriocáin	St Bricken's church
Luggacurren	Log an Churraigh	The hollow of the canoe
Mountmellick	Móinteach Mílic	Bogland of Mileac

Mountrath	Maighean Rátha	Steading of the ringfort
Portarlington (Eng.)	Cúil an tSúdaire	The tanner's recess
Portlaoise	Port Laoise	The fort of Laois
Rathdowney	Ráth Domhnaigh	Ringfort of the church
Rosenallis	Ros Fhionnghlaise	The wood of the white stream
Shanahoe	Seanchua	(obs.) Old corner?
Timahoe	Tigh Mochua	St Mochua's house

County Longford—*Contae Longfoirt*

Abbeylara	Mainistir Leathrátha	Monastery of the half-ringfort
Abbeyshrule	Mainistir Shruthla	Monastery of the stream
Ardagh	Ardach	Elevation
Aughnacliffe	Achadh na Cloiche	The field of the stone
Ballinalee	Béal Átha na Lao	The fordmouth of the calves
Ballinamuck	Béal Átha na Muc	The fordmouth of the swine
Ballymahon	Baile Uí Mhatháin	O Mathan's town
Barry	Barraigh	(obs.) Heights?
Carrickboy	An Charraig Buí	The yellow rock
Clondra	Cluain Dhá Ráth	Meadow of the two ringforts
Cloonagh	Cluain Each	Meadow of steeds
Colehill	Cnoc na Góla	(obs.) Forked hill?
Coolarty	Cúil Uí Fhathartaigh	Faherty's recess
Dring	Droing	(obs.) Humped hill?
Drumlish	Droim Lis	Ridge of the ringfort
Edgeworthstown (Eng.)	Meathas Troim	(obs.) Loss of weight?
Esker	An Eiscir	Esker
Granard	Gránard	(obs.) Tall grain?
Kenagh	Caonach	Peat-moss
Killashee	Cill na Sí	Church of the mound
Killoe	Cill Eo	Prince's church
Lanesborough (Eng.)	Béal Átha Liag	The fordmouth of the standing stones
Lenamore	An Léana Mór	The big water-meadow
Longford	An Longfort	Fortress

Moydow	Maigh Dumha	The plain of the mound
Moyne	An Mhaighean	The precinct
Newtown Cashel (Eng.)	Baile Nua an Chaisil	The new town of the stone fort
Newtownforbes (Eng.)	An Lios Breac	Speckled fort

County Louth—*Contae Lú*

Annagassan	Áth na gCasán	The ford of the paths
Ardee	Baile Átha Fhirdhia	The town of Ferdia's ford
Baltray	Baile Trá	Strandtown
Blackrock	Na Creagacha Dubha	The black rocks
Carlingford	Cairlinn	(Personal name)
Castlebellingham (Eng.)	Baile an Ghearlánaigh	O'Gearlan's town
Clogher Head	Ceann Chlochair	Head of the stony place
Collon	Collann	(obs.) Holly?
Corcreaghy	An Chorr Chríochach	(obs.) Finishing point?
Drogheda	Droichead Átha	Fordbridge
Dromin	Droim Ing	Ing's ridge
Dromiskin	Droim Ineasclainn	Ineasclann's ridge
Drumcar	Droim Chora	Weir-ridge
Dunany	Dún Áine	Anne's fort
Dundalk	Dún Dealgan	Dealgan's fort
Dunleer	Dún Léire	Leire's fort
Grangebellew (Eng.)	Gráinseach an Dísirt	Hermitage grange
Greenore	An Ghrianfort	Sunport
Hackballscross (Eng.)	Crois an Mhaoir	Myer's Cross
Kilcurley	Cill Choirle	Coirle's Church
Kilcurry	Cill an Churraigh	The church of the marsh
Knockbridge	Droichead an Chnoic	Hillbridge
Louth	Lú	(obs.)
Monasterboice	Mainistir Bhuithe	St Buithin's monastery
Omeath	Ó Méith	Descendant of Meith

Readypenny	Cillín Cúile	Recess church
Riverstown (Eng.)	Baile Nua	Newtown
Termonfeckin	Tearmann Feichín	St Feichin's sanctuary land
Togher	An Tóchar	The causeway
Tullyallen	Tulaigh Álainn	Lovely hillocks
Yellowbatter Park	Páirc an Bhóthair Bhuí	Park of the yellow road

County Meath—*Contae na Mí*

Agher	Achair	Journeys
An Uaimh	(formerly Navan)	The cave
Ashbourne (Eng.)	Cill Dhéagláin	St Declan's church
Athboy	Baile Átha Buí	The town of the yellow ford
Ballinabrackey	Buaile na Bréachmhaí	Breachmhai's milking-place
Ballinlough	Baile an Locha	The town of the lake
Ballivor	Baile Íomhair	Íomhar's town
Ballybeg	An Baile Beag	The little town
Balrath	Baile na Rátha	The town of the ringfort
Batterstown	Baile an Bhóthair	Road town
Bettystown	Baile an Bhiataigh	Victualler's town
Bohermeen	An Bóthar Mín	The smooth road
Boynagh	Buíonach	Treasured possession
Carnaross	Carn na Ros	Cairn of the woods
Ceanannas Mór	(formerly Kells)	(obscure)
Clonalvy	Cluain Ailbhe	Ailbhe's meadow
Clonard	Cluain Ioraird	Iorard's meadow
Clonee	Cluain Aodha	Hugh's meadow
Cortown	An Baile Corr	The odd town
Crossakiel	Crosa Caoil	Caol's crosses
Donaghpatrick	Domhnach Phádraig	St Patrick's church
Donore	Dún Uabhair	Fort of pride
Dowth	Dubhadh	(obs.) Place of darkness?
Drumconrath	Droim Conrach	Conrach's ridge
Drumone	Droim Eamhna	Eamhain's ridge

Drumree	Droim Rí	King's ridge
Duleek	Damhliag	Stone church
Dunboyne	Dún Búinne	Buinne's fort
Dunsany	Dún Samhnaí	Samhnach's fort
Dunshaughlin	Dún Seachlainn	St Secundinus' church
Enfield (Eng.)	An Bóthar Buí	The yellow road
Hayes (Eng.)	Carn Ulfa	Ulfa's cairn
Kilcarn	Cill an Chairn	The church of the cairn
Kilclone	Coill Chluana	The wood of the meadow
Kildalkey	Cill Dealga	Church of the thorn
Kilmainhamwood (Eng.)	Cill Mhaighneann	Maighne's church
Kilmessan	Cill Mheasáin	St Measan's church
Kilskyre	Cill Scíre	Scíre's church
Laytown (Eng.)	An Inse	The holm
Longwood (Eng.)	Maigh Dearmhaí	(obs.) Great plain?
Loughan	Lochán	Pool
Mosney	Maigh Muirí	Muirí's plain
Moynalty	Maigh nEalta	(obs.) Plain of the flock?
Nobber	An Obair	The work
Rathcore	Ráth Cuair	Hooped ringfort
Rathfeigh	Ráth Faiche	Ringfort of the green
Rathkenny	Ráth Cheannaigh	Ceannach's ringfort
Rathmolyon	Ráth Moliain	Molian's ringfort
Ratoath	Ráth Tó	To's ringfort
Ross	An Ros	The wood
Slane	Baile Shláine	(obs.) Health?
Stackallan	Stigh Colláin	(obs.) House of the body?
Stamullen	Steach Maoilín	(obs.) Maolan's house?
Tara	Teamhair	Lofty place
Teeworker	Taobh Urchair	Side of the cast
Trim	Baile Átha Troim	Town of the ford of the elder tree

County Offaly—*Contae Uíbh Failí*

Ballinagar	Béal Átha na gCarr	Ford-mouth of the cars
Ballycumber	Béal Átha Chomair	Ford-mouth of the ravine
Banagher	Beannchar	(obs.) Pinnacled place?
Belmont (Eng.)	An Lios Dearg	The red fort
Birr	Biorra	Watery place
Blue Ball (Eng.)	An Phailís	The palisade
Bracknagh	Breacánach	Speckled land
Brosna	An Bhrosnach	Kindling
Clara	Clóirtheach	Level place
Clareen	An Cláirín	The little plain
Cloghan	An Clochán	The stepping-stones
Clonbullogue	Cluain Bolg	Meadow of sacks
Cloneygowan	Cluain na nGamhan	Calf meadow
Clonfanlough	Cluain Fionnlocha	Meadow of the bright lake
Crinkle	Críonchoill	Withered wood
Croghan	Cruachán	Peak
Daingean	An Daingean	The fortress
Dunkerrin	Dún Cairin	Cairin's fort
Edenderry	Éadan Doire	Hill-brow of the oak-grove
Fahy	An Fhaiche	The green
Ferbane	An Féar Bán	The white grass
Five Alley	An Chúirt	The court
Fortel	Foirtil	Stronghold
Geashill	Géisill	Place of swans
Kilcormac	Cill Chormaic	Cormac's church

Killeigh	Cill Aichidh	Church of the field
Killurin	Cill Iúirín	Iúirín's church
Kinnitty	Cionn Eitigh	Eiteach's head
Moneygall	Muine Gall	Thicket of stones
Pollagh	Pollach	Hollow place
Rahan	Raithean	Place of ferns
Rhode	Ród	Road
Screggan	An Screagán	The rough ground
Sharavogue	Searbhóg	The bitter place
Shinrone	Suí an Róin	Seat of the hirsute man
Tullamore	Tulach Mhór	The big hill

County Westmeath—*Contae na hIarmhaí*

Athlone	Baile Átha Luain	The town of Luan's ford
Ballinagore	Béal Átha na nGabhar	The fordmouth of the goats
Ballinahowen	Buaile na hAbhann	River milking-place
Ballinalack	Béal Átha na Leac	The fordmouth of the flagstones
Ballinea	Béal an Átha	Fordmouth
Ballykeeran	Bealach Caorthainn	Rowan road
Ballymanus	Baile Mhánais	Manus's town
Ballymore	An Baile Mór	The big town
Ballynacargy	Baile na Carraige	The town of the rock
Baylin	Béal Linne	Poolmouth
Bunbrusna	Bun Brosnaí	Scrubby hill-base
Clonlost	Cluain Loiste	Meadow of the trough
Clonmellon (Eng.)	Ráistín	Shovel
Collinstown (Eng.)	Baile na gCailleach	The town of the nuns
Coole	An Chúil	The recess
Crooked Wood (Eng.)	Tigh Munna	Munna's church
Delvin	Dealbhna	The family of Dealbhna
Drumcree	Droim Cria	Ridge of cattle
Drumraney	Droim Raithne	Ferny ridge
Dysart	An Díseart	Hermitage
Finea	Fiodh an Átha	Fordwood
Fore	Baile Fhobhair	Spring
Gaybrook (Eng.)	Baile Réamainn	Raymond's town
Glasson	Glasán	Streamlet
Horseleap (Eng.)	Baile Átha an Urchair	The town of the ford of the cast

Kilbeggan	Cill Bheagháin	Beagan's church
Killucan	Cill Liúcainne	Lucan's church
Kinnegad	Cionn Átha Gad	Ford-head of the withes
Knockdrin	Cnoc Droinne	Hump-backed hill
Lismacaffrey	Lios Mhic Gofraidh	MacCaffrey's ringfort
Moate	An Móta	The mound
Monilea	An Muine Liath	The grey thicket
Mount Temple (Eng.)	An Grianán	Sun-palace
Moyvore	Maigh Mhórdha	Plain of Mordha
Moyvoughly	Maigh Bhachla	Plain of the bud
Mullingar	An Muillean cGearr	Wry mill
Multyfarnham	Muilte Farannáin	Farannan's mills
Raharney	Ráth Fhearna	Ringfort of the alder
Rathconrath	Ráth Conarta	Conarta's ringfort
Rathowen	Ráth Eoghain	Eoghan's ringfort
Rochfort Bridge (Eng.)	Droichead Chaisleáin Loiste	Bridge of the castle lodge
Rosemount (Eng.)	Baile an Bhric Oig	Town of the young trout
Slanemore	Sleamhain Mhór	The great elm
Tang	An Teanga	The tongue

County Wexford—*Contae Loch Garman*

Adamstown	Maigh Arnaí	Hard plain
Annagh Cross	Crois an Eanaigh	The cross of the marsh
Askamore	An Easca Mhór	The big bog
Ballindaggin	Baile an Daingin	The fortified town
Ballycanew	Baile Uí Chonnmhaí	Conway's town
Ballycarney	Baile Uí Chearnaigh	Carney's town
Ballycogley	Baile Uí Choigligh	Quigley's town
Ballycullane	Baile Uí Choileáin	Collins' town
Ballyfadd	An Baile Fada	Long town
Ballygarrett	Baile Ghearóid	Gerard's town
Ballyhogue	Baile Uí Cheog	Hogue's town
Ballymitty	Baile Uí Mhitigh	Mitty's town
Ballymoney	Baile Muine	Town of the thicket
Ballymurn	Baile Uí Mhurúin	Murren's town
Ballywiliam	Baile Liam	William's town
Barntown	Baile an Bharúnaigh	Baron's town
Boolavogue	Buaile Mhaodhóg	Maodhog's milking-place
Bree	Brí	Hill
Broadway (Eng.)	Gráinseach Iúir	Yew-tree grange
Bunclody	Bun Clóidí	The mouth of the Clody (river)
Camolin	Cam Eolaing	Eolang's bend
Campile	Ceann Poill	Head of the creek
Carrick	An Charraig	The rock
Clohamon	Cloch Ámainn	Amann's stone
Clonroche	Cluain an Róistigh	Roche's meadow

Coolgreany	Cúil Ghréine	Sunny recess
Craanford (Eng.)	Áth an Chorráin	Ford of the sickle
Crossabeg	Na Crosa Beaga	The little crosses
Curracloe	Currach Cló	Cló's marsh
Duncannon	Dún Canann	(obs.) Canann's fort?
Duncormick	Dún Chormaic	Cormac's fort
Enniscorthy	Inis Córthaidh	Corthaidh's holm
Ferns	Fearna	Place of alders
Fethard	Fiodh Ard	High wood
Glenbryan	Gleann Bhriain	Brian's valley
Gorey	Guaire	Sandbank
Inch	An Inis	The holm
Kilanerin	Coill an Iarainn	Ironwood
Kilcotty	Cill Chota	Cota's church
Killanne	Cill Anna	St Anna's church
Killena	Cill Éanach	Eanach's church
Killinick	Cill Fhionnóg	Fionnog's church
Killurin	Cill Liúráin	Liuran's church
Kilmore	An Chill Mhór	The big church
Kilmuckridge	Cill Mhucraise	St Muchraise's church
Kilrane	Cill Ruáin	Church of the red-haired person
Kiltealy	Cill Téile	Teal's church
Monamolin	Muine Moling	St Moling's thicket
Murrintown	Baile Mhúráin	St Muran's church
New Ross (Eng.)	Ros Mhic Thriúin	The wood of Triun's son
Oulart	An tAbhallort	The orchard
Oylgate (Eng.)	Maolán na nGabhar	The smooth hill of the goats
Raheen	An Ráithín	The little ringfort
Rathnure	Ráth an Iúir	Yew ringfort
Rosslare	Ros Láir	Middle headland
Screen	An Scrín	The shrine
Slade	An Slaod	The swathe

Leinster—*Cúige Laighean*

Strahart	Sraith Airt	Art's spreading-place
Taghmon	Teach Munna	Munna's house
Tagoat	Teach Gót	Got's house
The Ballagh	An Bealach	The highway
Tomhaggard	Teach Moshagard	Moshagard's house
Wexford (Eng.)	Loch Garman	Inlet of the Garma (river)

County Wicklow—*Contae Chill Mhantáin*

Annamoe	Áth na mBó	The ford of the cows
Arklow (Eng.)	An tInbhear Mór	The big estuary
Ashford (Eng.)	Áth na Fuinseoige	Ashford
Aughrim	Eachroim	(obs.) Horse ridge?
Avoca	Abhóca	(obs.)
Ballinglen	Baile an Ghleanna	Town of the glen
Ballycooge	Baile Chuag	(obs.) Cuag's town?
Baltinglass	Bealach Conglais	Conglas's road
Blessington (Eng.)	Baile Coimín	Comyn's town
Bray	Bré	(obs.) Hill?
Brittas Bay	Cuan an Bhriotáis	The harbour of the brattice
Carnew	Carn an Bhua	The cairn of the victory
Clash	An Chlais	The trench
Coolboy	An Cúl Buí	The yellow recess
Coolkenno	Cúil Uí Chionaoith	O'Cionaoith's recess
Delgany	Deilgne	Thorny place
Donard	Dún Árd	High fort
Dunlavin	Dún Lúain	Halo fort
Enniskerry	Áth na Sceire	Ford of the reef
Glendalough	Gleann dá Loch	The valley of the two lakes
Gleanealy	Gleann Fhaidhle	Faidhle's valley
Grangecon	Gráinseach Choinn	Grange of wisdom
Hollywood	Cillín Chaoimhín	St Kevin's cell
Kilbride	Cill Bhríde	St Brigid's church
Kilcoole	Cill Chomhghaill	St Comgall's church

Kilmacanogue	Cill Mocheanóg	St Mocheanog's church
Kilranelagh	Cill Rannaileach	St Randall's church
Kiltegan	Cill Téagáin	St Teagan's church
Knockanna	Cnoc an Eanaigh	The hill of the fen
Knockanarrigan	Cnoc an Aragain	(obs.) Ledge hill?
Knockrath	Cnoc Rátha	Ringfort hill
Lacken	An Leacain	Scree
Moneystown	An Muine	The thicket
Moyne	An Mhaighean	The precinct
Mullinacuffe	Muileann Mhic Dhuibh	MacDuff's mill
Newtownmount-kennedy (Eng.)	Baile an Chinnéidigh	Kennedy's town
Newtown Vevay (Eng.)	An tSeanchúirt	The old court
Rathdangan	Ráth Daingin	Ringfort of the stronghold
Rathdrum	Ráth Droma	Ringfort of the ridge
Rathnew	Ráth Naoi	Naoi's ringfort
Roundwood (Eng.)	An Tóchar	The causeway
Shillelagh	Síol Éalaigh	The seed of Ealach
Tinahely	Tigh na hÉille	House of the fork
Wicklow (Scand.)	Cill Mhantáin	Mantan's church

Munster—*Cúige Mumhan*

County Clare—*Contae an Chláir*

Ardnacrusha	Ard na Croise	The height of the cross
Ballanruan	Baile an Ruáin	The town of the red-haired person
Ballynacally	Baile na Caillí	The town of the nun
Ballyvaughan	Baile Uí Bheacháin	O'Beachain's town
Bodyke	Lúbán Díge	Dyke loop
Burrin	Boirinn	Stony places
Caher	An Chathair	The stone fort
Carrahan	Carrachán	(obs.) Large rock?
Carrigaholt	Carraig an Chabhaltaigh	The rock of the fleet
Carron	An Carn	The cairn
Clonlara	Cluain Lára	Mare meadow
Clonroadmore	Cluain Ráda	(obs.) Rad's meadow?
Connolly (Eng.)	Fíoch Rua	Red village
Coolmeen	Cúil Mhín	Level recess
Cooraclare	Cuar an Chláir	Curve of the plain
Corofin	Cora Finne	Finn's weir
Craggagh	An Chreagach	Rocky (place)
Cranny	An Chrannaigh	The stake fence
Cratloe	An Chreatalach	The framework
Cree	An Chríoch	The boundary
Crusheen	An Croisín	The little cross
Darragh	An Darach	The oak tree
Doolin	Dúlainn	(obs.) Black church?
Doonaha	Dún Átha	Ford fort

Doonbeg	An Dún Beag	The little fort
Doonogan	Dún Ógáin	Ogan's fort
Dromindoora	Drom an Dúdhoire	Ridge of the dark oakgrove
Drumgeely	Drom Gaibhle	Fork ridge
Dunsallagh	Dún Salach	Willow fort
Ennis	Inis	Holm
Ennistymon	Inis Díomáin	Dioman's holm
Feakle	An Fhiacail	The tooth
Flagmount (Eng.)	Leacain an Éadain	Scree of the hill-brow
Fountain Cross (Eng.)	Tobar Mháille	Maille's well
Inagh	Eidhneach	(Place of) ivy
Kilbaha	Cill Bheathach	Birch church
Kilbane	An Choill Bhán	The white wood
Kildysart	Cill an Dísirt	The church of the hermitage
Kilfenora	Cill Fhionnúrach	Church of Fionnuir
Kilkee	Cill Chaoi	St Chaoi's church
Kilkishen	Cill Chisín	Church of the little wicker causeway
Killaloe	Cill Dalua	St Dalua's church
Killmaley	Cill Mháille	Maille's church
Killmihil	Cill Mhichíl	St Michael's church
Kilmore	An Chill Mhór	The big church
Kilmurry	Cill Mhuire	Church of Our Lady
Kilmurry McMahon	Cill Mhuire Mhic Mathúna	McMahon's church of Our Lady
Kilnaboy	Cill Iníne Baoith	Church of the daughter of Baoth
Kilnamona	Cill na Móna	The church of the peat
Kilrush	Cill Rois	Church of the wood
Kilshanny	Cill Seanaigh	Seanach's church
Knock	An Cnoc	The hill
Knockalough	Cnoc an Locha	The hill of the lake
Labasheeda	Leaba Shíoda	Sioda's bed
Lahinch	An Leacht	The gravemound
Liscannor	Lios Ceannúir	Ceannur's ringfort

Lisdeen	Lios Duibhinn	Duibheann's ringfort
Lisdoonvarna	Lios Dúin Bhearna	The enclosure of the gap ringfort
Lissycasey	Lios Uí Chathasaigh	O'Casey's ringfort
Miltown Malbay (Eng.)	Sráid na Cathrach	The village of the stone fort
Mountshannon (Eng.)	Baile Uí Bheoláin	Boland's town
Moyasta	Maigh Sheasta	Seasta's plain
Mullagh	Mullach	Hilltop
Newmarket-on-Fergus	Cora Chaitlín	Kathleen's weir (Eng.)
Ogonnelloe	Tuath Ó gConaíle	Connolly's tribe
Querrin	An Cuibhreann	The tilled field
Quilty	Coillte	Woods
Quin	Cuinche	(obs.) Quince?
Scarriff	An Scairbh	The shallow
Shanahae	Seanachae	(obs.) Old field?
Sixmilebridge	Droichead Abhann Ó gCearnaigh	Kearneys' Riverbridge
Tiermaclane	Tír Mhic Calláin	Mac Callan's land
Tuamgraney	Tuaim Gréine	The gravemound of Grian
Tulla	An Tulach	The hillock

County Cork—*Contae Chorcaí*

Adrigole	Eadargóil	Place between two rivers
Aghabullogue	Achadh Bolg	Field of the sacks
Aghadown	Achadh Dúin	Field of the fort
Aghinagh	Achadh Fhíonach	Wine field
Aherla	An Eatharla	(obs.) Ferryboats?
Allihies	Na hAilichí	The rocky places
Araglin	Airglinn	(Obs.) Airy glen?
Ardfield	Ard Ó bhFicheallaigh	O'Feely's height
Ardgroom	Dhá Dhrom	Two ridges
Ballinacarriga	Béal na Carraige	Mouth of the rock
Ballinaclashet	Baile na Claise	Town of the gully
Ballinacurra	Baile na Cora	Town of the weir
Ballinadee	Baile na Daibhche	Town of the pool
Ballinagree	Baile na Graí	Town of the horses
Ballinamona	Baile na Móna	Town of the turf
Ballinascarthy	Baile na Scairte	Town of the thicket
Ballincollig	Baile an Chollaigh	Town of the boar
Ballincurrig	Baile an Churraigh	Town of the marsh
Ballindangan	Baile an Daingin	Town of the stronghold
Ballineen	Béal Átha Fhínín	Town of the fordmouth of Finin
Ballingeary	Béal Átha an Ghaorthaidh	Fordmouth of the river bed
Ballinhassig	Béal Átha an Cheasaigh	Fordmouth of the wooden causeway
Ballinlough	Baile an Locha	Town of the lake
Ballinspittle	Béal Átha an Spidéil	Fordmouth of the hospital

Munster—*Cúige Mumhan*

Ballintemple	Baile an Teampaill	Town of the church
Ballyclough	Baile Cloch	Town of the stone
Ballycotton	Baile Choitín	Town of the small boat
Ballydaheen	Baile Dáithín	Town of little David
Ballydehob	Béal an Dá Chab	Twin mouth (of river)
Ballyfeard	Baile Feá Aird	Town of the tall beech tree
Ballygarvan	Baile Garbháin	Town of St Garvan
Ballyhooly	Baile Átha hÚlla	Town of the ford of the apple
Ballylickey	Béal Átha Leice	Fordmouth of the flagstone
Ballymacoda	Baile Mhac Óda	Town of Magillacuddy
Ballymakeera	Baile Mhic Íre	Town of the son of Ire
Ballynoe	Baile Nua	Newtown
Ballyphehane	Baile Féitheán	Guard town
Ballyvoige	Baile Uí Bhuaigh	O'Boag's town
Ballyvourney	Baile Bhuirne	The town in the stony district
Baltimore (Eng.)	Dún na Séad	Fort of the jewels
Bandon	Droichead na Bandan	Bridge of the Bandon river
Banteer	Bántír	White land
Bantry	Beanntraí	Tribe of Beann
Barrackton (Eng.)	Gleann Ciotáin	Glen of the little boat
Bartlemy (Eng.)	Tobar Pártnáin	Partnan's well
Belgooly	Béal Guala	Shoulder pass
Belvelly	Béal an Bhealaigh	Mouth of the pass
Blarney	An Bhlarna	Exposed place
Boherbue	An Bóthar Buí	The yellow road
Buttevant (Eng.)	Cill na Mallach	Church of the mound
Bweeng	Na Boinn	(obs.) Coins?
Caheragh	Cathrach	Place of stone forts
Cahermore	Cathair Mhór	Large stone fort
Carrigaline	Carraig Uí Leighin	Lyons's rock
Carriganimmy	Carraig an Ime	Butter rock
Carrignavar	Carraig na bhFear	Men's rock
Carrigrohane	Carraig Ruacháin	Roughan's rock

Carrigtwohill	Carraig Thuathail	Tuathal's rock
Castlecor	Caisleán na Cora	Castle of the weir
Castlefreke (Eng.)	Ráth an Bharraigh	Stonefort of the height
Castletown Kinneigh	Baile Chaisleáin Chinn Eich	The castle of the town abounding in horses
Cecilstown (Eng.)	Baile an Bhriotaigh	The town of the lisper
Church Cross	Cnoc na Rátha	Hill of the ringforts
Clonakilty	Cloch na Coillte	The stone of the straits
Clondrohid	Cluain Droichead	Meadow of the bridges
Cloyne	Cluain	Meadow
Cóbh	An Cóbh	Cove
Conna	Conaithe	Dwellings
Coolea	Cúil Aodha	Huch's recess
Coppeen	An Caipín	Top
Cork	Corcaigh	Marsh
Crookhaven	An Cruachán	Little round hill
Crookstown	An Baile Gallda	English town
Crossbarry	Crois an Bharraigh	The cross at the summit
Crosshaven	Bun an Tábhairne	Lowland of the tavern
Cullen	Cuillinn	Holly
Currabeha	An Chorr Bheithe	The bend of the beech tree
Curraglass	Cora Ghlas	Green hill
Derinacarah	Doirín na Cathrach	Litle oakgrove of the stone fort
Derinagree	Doire na Graí	Oakgrove of the horses
Desertserges	An Díseart	The hermitage
Doneraile	Dún ar Aill	Cliff fort
Donoughmore	Domhnach Mór	Big church
Drimoleague	Drom Dhá Liag	Ridge of the two pillar stones
Drinagh	Draighneach	Thorny thicket
Dripsey	An Druipseach	Muddy river
Dromina	Drom Aidhne	(obs.) Aidhne's ridge
Drommahane	Drom Átháin	(obs.) Ridge of the ford
Dunderrow	Dún Darú	Daru's fort

Dungourney	Dún Guairne	Guairne's fort
Dunmanway	Dún Mánmhaí	Fort of Manmha's teritory
Durrus	Dúras	Black wood
Dursey Island (Eng.)	Oileán Baoi	Buoy Island
Enniskean	Inis Céin	Distant island
Eyeries	Na hAoraí	The shepherds
Farnanes	Na Fearnáin	The alder
Farran	An Fearann	Land
Farranhavane	Fearann Uí Chiabháin	Land of the Caomhans
Farranree	Fearann an Rí	King's land
Fermoy	Mainistir Fhear Maí	Monastery of the plainsmen
Freemount (Eng.)	Cillín an Chrónáin	The little church of St Cronan
Gaggin	Géagánach	Branchy place
Garnish	Garinis	Near island
Glandore	Cuan Dor	Dor's harbour
Glanmire	Gleann Maghair	Glen of the plain
Glantane	An Gleanntán	Little glen
Glanworth	Gleannúir	Glen of the yew
Glengarriff	An Gleann Garbh	Rough glen
Glenlough	Gleann Locha	Lake glen
Glenville (Eng.)	Gleann an Phréacháin	Crow's glen
Glounthaune	An Gleanntán	Little glen
Goleen	Góilín	Little inlet
Gortroe	Gort an Rú	The field of rue
Grenagh	Greanach	Sandy place
Gurranebraher	Garrán na mBráthar	The brothers garden
Haulbowline (Eng.)	Inis Sionnach	Foxes' Island
Inchigeelagh	Inse Geimhleach	Prisoners island
Inniscarra	Inis Cara	Island of the leg
Innishannon	Inis Eonáin	Holm of Eonan
Johnstown (Eng.)	Cill Sheanaigh	St Senan's Church
Kanturk	Ceann Toirc	Headland of the boar
Kealkill	An Chaolchoill	The narrow wood

Keimaneigh	Céim an Fhia	Deer's leap
Kilbarry	Cill Barra	Church of St Finbar
Kilbrittain	Cill Briotáin	St Briotan's church
Kilbrogan	Cill Brógáin	St Brogan's church
Kilcorney	Cill Coirne	St Coirne's church
Kildinan	Cill Daighnín	Church of the stronghold
Kildorrery	Cill Dairbhre	Church of the oaks
Killavullen	Cill an Mhuilinn	Church of the mill
Killeagh	Cill Ia	St Ia's church
Killinardrish	Cill an Ard-dorais	Church of the high door
Kilmichael	Cill Mhichíl	St Michael's church
Kilmurry	Cill Muire	Mary's church
Kilworth	Cill Uird	Church of the order
Kinsale	Cionn tSáile	Head of the sea
Kiskeam	Coiscéim na Caillí	Hag's step
Knockanevin	Cnocán Aoibhinn	Lovely hill
Knocknagree	Cnoc na Graí	Hill of the horses
Knockraha	Cnoc Rátha	Hill of the ringforts
Lady's Bridge (Eng.)	Droichead na Scuab	Brush bridge
Leap	An Léim	The leap
Lemlara	Léim Lára	Mare's leap
Lisbealad	Lios Béalaid	Béalad's ringfort
Liscarroll	Lios Cearúill	Carroll's ringfort
Lislevane	Lios Leamháin	Ringfort of the elmtree
Lissacreasig	Lios an Chraosaigh	Ringfort of the gorge
Lissarda	Lios Ardachaidh	Ringfort of the high field
Lyre	An Ladhar	River-fork
Macroom	Maigh Chromtha	Sloping plain
Mallow	Mala	Plain of the rock
Meelin	An Mhaoilinn	The bleak eminence
Midleton	Mainistir na Corann	The monastery of the weir
Minane Bridge	Droichead an Mhionnáin	The bridge of the pointed rock
Mogeely	Maigh Dhíle	Flood plain

Mount Uniacke (Eng.)	Cúil O gCorra	Corr's recess
Myrtleville (Eng.)	Baile an Chuainín	Town of the little bay
Newcestown (Eng.)	Baile Níos	Nios's town
Newmarket (Eng.)	Áth Trasna	Ford on the other side
Newtownballyhea	Bealach Átha	Highroad of the ford
Nohoval	Nuachabháil	New ruins
Ovens	Na hUamhanna	The caves
Poulanargid	Poll an Airgid	Hole of the money
Rathcoole	Ráth Cúil	Ringfort of the recess
Rathcormac	Ráth Chormaic	Cormac's ringfort
Charleville (Eng.)	Ráth Luirc	Lorc's ringfort
Reenascreena	Rae na Scríne	Plain of the shrine
Renanirree	Rae na nDoirí	Plain of the oakgrove
Rerrin	Raerainn	Part of the plain
Ringaskiddy	Rinn an Scídigh	Skiddy's point
Riverstick	Áth an Mhaide	Ford of the stick
Rosscarbery	Ros O gCairbre	The wood of the O'Cairbres
Rossmacowen	Ros Mhic Eoghain	The wood of the son of Eoghan
Rossmore	An Ros Mór	Large promontory
Rostellan	Ros Tialláin	Dillon's wood
Rylane	Réileán	Dancing field
Schull	An Scoil	The school
Shanagarry	An Seangharraí	The old field
Shanbally	An Seanbhaile	The old town
Shanballymore	An Seanbhaile Mór	The big old town
Shanlaragh	Seanlárach	Old site
Sherkin	Inis Arcáin	Arcan's island
Skibbereen	An Sciobairín	Place of little boats
Tarelton	Tír Eiltín	Hind country
Taur	Teamhair	Lofty place
Templemartin	Teampall Mártan	Church of Martin
Timoleague	Tigh Molaige	St Molaige's house
Toames	Tuaim	Grave mound

Togher	An Tóchar	The causeway
Toormore	An Tuar Mór	The big field
Trafrask	Trá Phraisce	Muddy strand
Tullylease	Tulach Léis	Bright mound
Union Hall (Eng.)	Bréantrá	Foul strand
Upton	Garraí Thancaird	Tancred's garden
Urhan	Iorthan	(obs.) Promontory?
Waterfall	Tobar an Iarla	The Earl's well
Watergrasshill (Eng.)	Cnocán na Biolrái	The hill of the cress
Whiddy Island	Faoide	(obs.) Bad weather
Youghal	Eochaill	Yew wood

County Kerry—*Contae Chiarraí*

Abbeydorney	Mainistir Ó dTorna	The abbey of the people of Torna
Aghadoe	Achadh Dá Eo	Field of the two yews
Aghatubrid	Achadh Tiobraid	Well field
Annascaul	Abhainn an Scáil	The river of the hero
Ardfert	Ard Fhearta	The height of the graves
Asdee	Eas Daoi	Embankment waterfall
Ballinskelligs	Baile an Sceilg	The town of the Skellig rock
Ballybunion	Baile an Bhuinneánaigh	The town of Bunyan
Ballydavid	Baile na nGall	The town of the foreigners
Ballyduff	An Baile Dubh	The black town
Ballyferriter	Baile an Fheirtéaraigh	The town of the Ferriters
Ballyhar	Baile Uí Aichir	The town of Aichear
Ballyheigue	Baile Ui Thaidhg	The town of the family of Tadhg
Ballylongford	Béal Átha Longfoirt	The fordmouth of the fort
Ballymacelligott	Baile Mhic Eileagóid	The town of the MacElligots
Ballymullen	Baile an Mhuilinn	The town of the mill
Banemore	An Bán Mór	The great bawn
Beaufort	Lios an Phúca	The fort of the fairies
Blennerville (Eng.)	Cathair Uí Mhóráin	Moran's fort
Bonane	An Bunán	The stump
Brandon	Cé Bhréanainn	St Brendan's Quay
Brosna	Brosnach	The place of the kindling
Caherconree	Cathair Conraoi	The fort of Conraoi
Caherdaniel	Cathair Dónaill	The fort of Daniel
Cahirciveen	Cathair Saidhbhín	Little Sadhbh's stone fort

Camp	An Com	Coomb
Caragh Lake	Loch Cárthaí	The lake of the McCarthys
Castlemaine	Caisleán na Mainge	The castle of the river Maine
Chapeltown (Eng.)	An Caol	The strait
Cloghane	An Clochán	Stepping Stones
Clonkeen	Cluain Chaoin	Pleasant meadow
Cordal	Cordal	(obs.)The level place ?
Cromane	An Cromán	The crow (place of)
Currow	Corra	The twisty place
Dingle	An Daingean	The stonghold
Duagh	Dubháth	Black ford
Dunquin	Dún Chaoin	The pleasant fort
Emlaghmore	An tImleach Mór	The big piece of marshy land
Faha	Faiche	The lea
Farranfore	An Fearann Fuar	The cold land
Fenit	An Fhianait	The wild place
Firies	Na Foidhrí	The hollows
Fybagh	An Fhadhbach	Uneven land
Gap of Dunloe (Eng)	Bearna an Choimín	The gap of the commons
Glenbeigh	Gleann Beithe	Glen of the beech trees
Glencar	Gleann Chárthaigh	Glen of the McCarthys
Glenderry	Gleann Doire	Glen of the oak wood
Glenflesk	Gleann Fleisce	Glen of the Rod
Gneeveguilla	Gníomh go Leith	Land measure (and a half)
Gortatlea	Gort an tSléibhe	The mountain field
Great Blasket, The	An Blascaod Mór	(obs)
Greenane	Grianán	Sunny dwelling
Headford	Lios na gCeann	The highest fort
Inch	Inse	Holm
Inis na Bró	Inis na Bró	Dense island
Inis Tuaisceart	Inis Tuaisceart	North Island
Kells	Na Cealla	Monastic cells
Kenmare (Eng.)	Neidín	Little nest

70

Munster—*Cúige Mumhan*

Kielduff	An Chill Dubh	The black church
Kilcummin	Cill Chuimín	The church of the common land
Kilflynn	Cill Flainn	The church of St Flann
Kilgarvan	Cill Gharbháin	The church of St Garbhan
Kilgobnet	Cill Ghobnait	The church of St Gobnait
Killarney	Cill Airne	The fort of the sloes
Kllorglin	Cill Orglan	The church of St Orgla
Kilmorna	Coill Mhaonaigh	The wood of Morna
Kilmoyley	Cill Mhaoile	The church of the round hill
Knocknagashel	Cnoc na gCaiseal	Hill of the forts
Lauragh	An Láithreach	Site
Lisbaby	Lios Báibe	(obs.) Baidhh's ringfort
Lispole	Lios Póil	Paul's ringfort
Lisselton	Lios Eiltín	The fort of the hind
Listowel	Lios Tuathail	Tuathal's ringfort
Lixnaw	Leic Snámha	Flag
Loughguitane	Loch Coiteáin	Lake of the little boat
Lyracrompane	Ladhar an Chrompáin	River fork of the creek
Magharees, The	Oileáin an Mhacaire	Spits
Moyvane	Maigh Mheáin	The central plain
Muckross	Mucros	Pig's headland
Portmagee	An Caladh	The pier
Rathmore	An Ráth Mhór	The big ringfort
Scartaglen	Scairteach an Ghlinne	The glen thicket
Shronowen	Srón Abhann	River promontory
Slea Head	Ceann Sléibhe	The mountainous headland
Sliabh Luachra	Sliabh Luachra	Mountain of rushes
Smerwick (Eng.)	Ard na Caithne	Height of the arbutus tree
Sneem	An tSnaidhm	The knot
Stradbally	An tSráidbhaile	The village
Tahilla	Tathuile	(obs.) Place of floods
Tarbert	Tairbeart	Peninsula
Tralee	Trá Lí	Strand of Lí

Valentia Island	Dairbhre	Island of the oaks
Ventry	Ceann Trá	The head of the beach
Waterville (Eng.)	An Coireán	The little whirlpool

County Limerick—Contae Luimnigh

Abbeyfeale	Mainistir na Féile	Abbey of the Feale (river)
Adare	Áth Dara	Ford of the oak
Anglesborough (Eng.)	Gleann na gCreabhar	The valley of woodcock
Ardagh	Ardach	Elevation
Ardpatrick	Ard Pádraig	St Patrick's height
Askeaton	Eas Géitine	The cascade of Geitine
Athlacca	An tÁth Leacach	Flagstone ford
Ballagh	An Bealach	Highroad
Ballingarry	Baile an Gharraí	The town of the garden
Ballingrane	Baile an Gharráin	The town of the grove
Ballyagran	Béal Átha Grean	Gritty fordmouth
Ballyhahill	Baile dhá Thuile	Twin-flood town
Ballylanders	Baile an Londraigh	(obs.) Shining town?
Ballynantybeg	Baile Uí Neachtain Beag	Town of the Naughton Begs
Banogue	An Bhánóg	The green patch
Brittas	An Briotás	The brattice
Broadford	Béal an Átha	The mouth of the ford
Bruff	An Brú	Hostel
Bruree	Brú Rí	King's hostel
Bulgaden	Builgidín	(obs.) Corpulent person?
Caherconlish	Cathair Chinn Lis	Fort of the head of Lis
Caherelly	Cathair Ailí	Rocky fortress
Cahirdavin	Cathair Dhaibhín	Davin's fortress
Cappamore	An Cheapach Mhór	The large plot of land
Carrigkerry	Carraig Chiarraí	Kerry rock

Castlemahon	Caisleán Maí Tamhnach	Castle of the green plain
Castletroy	Caladh an Treoigh	(Obs.) The landing-place?
Clarina	Clár Aidhne	Aidhne's plain
Cloncagh	Cluain Cath	Battle meadow
Crecora	Craobh Chomhartha	Marked branch
Croagh	Cróch	Crocus
Croom	Cromadh	Bend
Doon	Dún	Fort
Dromacomer	Drom an Chomair	The ridge of the ravine
Dromkeen	Drom Caoin	Pleasant ridge
Drumcollogher	Drom Collachair	Ridge of the hazel wood
Elton	Eiltiún	(obs.)Little doe
Feenagh	Fíonach	(obs.)Place rich in wine?
Feohanagh	An Fheothanach	Breezy place
Galbally	An Gallbhaile	The foreigners' town
Garrydoolis	Garraí Dúlas	Dulas's garden
Garryfine	Garraí Phaghain	Paghan's garden
Garryspillane	Garraí Uí Spealáin	Spillane's garden
Glenroe	An Gleann Rua	The red valley
Glin	An Gleann	The valley
Granagh	Greanach	(Place of) gravelly soil
Holycross (Eng.)	Baile na gCailleach	The town of the nuns
Kilbehenny	Coill Bheithne	Birch wood
Kilcolman	Cill Cholmáin	St Colman's church
Kildimo	Cill Díoma	St Dioma's church
Kilfinane	Cill Fhíonáin	St Fionan's church
Kilmallock	Cill Mocheallóg	St Mocheallog's church
Kilmeedy	Cill Míde	St Mide's church
Kilteely	Cill Tíle	(obs.) Sile's church?
Knockaderry	Cnoc an Doire	The hill of the oakgrove
Knockainy	Cnoc Áine	Anne's hill
Knocklong	Cnoc Loinge	The hill of the house
Limerick	Luimneach	(obs.)
Lisnagry	Lios na Graí	The fort of the horses

Munster—*Cúige Mumhan*

Loughill	Leamhchoill	Blighted wood
Manister	Mainistir	Abbey
Murroe	Maigh Rua	Red plain
Oola	Úlla	Apples
Pallasgreen	Pailís Ghréine	Grian's palisade
Pallaskenry	Pailís Chaonraí	Caonrai's palisade
Rathkeale	Ráth Caola	Caola's ringfort
Reens	Roighne	Choices
Shanagolden	Seanghualainn	Old hill-shoulder
Templeglantine	Teampall an Ghleanntáin	The church of the little valley
Tournafulla	Tuar na Fola	Bleachgreen of the hedges

County Tipperary—*Contae Thiobraid Árann*

Aglish	An Eaglais	The church
Ahenny	Áth Eine	Eine's ford
Aherlow	Eatharlach	Valley
Annacarty	Áth na Cairte	The fort of the charts
Ardcroney	Ard Cróine	Crón's height
Ardfinnan	Ard Fhíonáin	St Fíonán's height
Ballinaclough	Baile na Cloiche	Town of the stone
Ballinahinch	Baile na hInse	Town of the holm
Ballinard	Baile an Aird	Town of the hillock
Ballinderry	Baile an Doire	The town of the oakgrove
Ballingarry	Baile an Gharraí	The town of the garden
Ballinure	Baile an Iúir	Town of the yew
Ballycahill	Bealach Achaille	The Achaille road
Ballycommon	Baile Uí Chomáin	O'Coman's town
Ballylooby	Béal Átha Lúbaigh	The mouth of the looped ford
Ballymackey	Baile Uí Mhacaí	Mackey's town
Ballyneal	Baile Uí Néill	O'Neill's town
Ballypatrick	Baile Phádraig	St Patrick's town
Ballyporeen	Béal Átha Póirín	Fordmouth of the pebbles
Bansha	An Bháinseach	Grassy place
Barna	Bearna	Gap
Birdhill (Eng.)	Cnocán an Éin Fhinn	Knoll of the white bird
Boherlahan	An Bóthar Leathan	The broad road
Borrisokane	Buiríos Uí Chéin	O'Cein's borough
Borrisoleigh	Buiríos Ó Luigheach	Borough of the Luigeachs

Munster—*Cúige Mumhan*

Bouladuff	An Bhuaile Dhubh	The black milking-place
Cahir	An Chathair	The stone fort
Capparoe	An Cheapach Rua	The red tillage plot
Carney	Carnaigh	Place of cairns
Carrick-on-Suir	Carraig na Siúire	Rock of the Suir (river)
Carrigahorig	Carraig an Chomhraic	The rock of the fight
Carrigatoher	Carraig an Tóchair	The rock of the causeway
Cashel	Caiseal	Stone fort
Castleiney	Caisleán Laighnigh	Leinster castle
Clerihan	Baile Uí Chléireacháin	O'Cleireachán's town
Clogheen	An Chloichín	The little stone
Clonmel	Cluain Meala	Honey meadow
Cloughjordan	Cloch Shiurdáin	Jordan's stone
Coolbawn	An Cúl Bán	The white recess
Cullen	Cuilleann	Holly
Curraguneen	Currach Guinín	Guinin's marsh
Curreeney	Na Coirríní	(obs.) The little hollows?
Dolla	An Doladh	The grief
Donohill	Dún Eochaille	Yew fort
Dovea	An Dubhfhéith	The black seam
Drangan	Drongán	Hunchback
Drom	An Drom	The ridge
Drombane	An Drom Bán	The white ridge
Dromineer	Drom Inbhir	Estuary ridge
Dundrum	Dún Droma	Fort of the ridge
Emly	Imleach	Lake border
Fethard	Fiodh Ard	High forest
Golden	An Gabhailín	The little (river-)fork
Gurtnahoe	Gort na hUamha	The field of the cave
Holycross (Eng.)	Mainistir na Croiche	Abbey of the cross
Horse and Jockey (Eng.)	An Marcach	The rider
Kilcommon	Cill Chuimín	Cuimin's church
Killea	Cill Shléibhe	Mountain church

Killenaule	Cill Náile	Naile's church
Killoscully	Cill Ó Scolaí	O'Scully's church
Kilross	Cill Ros	Church of the woods
Kilsheelan	Cill Síoláin	Síolán's church
Knock	An Cnoc	The hill
Knockbrett	Cnoc an Bhriotaigh	Briotach's hill
Lackamore	An Leaca Mhór	The big hillside
Latteragh	Leatracha	Hillsides
Lisronagh	Lios Ruanach	Ruddy fort
Lisvernane	Lios Fearnáin	Alder fort
Lorrha	Lothra	(obs.) Semicircular structure?
Loughmore	Luachma	(obs.) Valuable place?
Moyne	An Mhaighean	The steading
Mullinahone	Muileann na hUamhan	The mill of the cave
Nenagh	An tAonach	The fair
New Birmingham (Eng.)	Gleann an Ghuail	Valley of coal
New Inn (Eng.)	Loch Ceann	Head lake
Portroe	An Port Rua	The red fort
Puckane	Pocán	Bag
Rathcabbin	Ráth Cabáin	Ringfort of the cabin
Rathkea	Ráth Cae	The ringfort of the ditch
Rearcross	Crois na Rae	Row cross
Riverstown (Eng.)	Baile Uí Lachnáin	O'Lachnán's town
Roscrea	Ros Cré	Cre's wood
Rossadrehid	Ros an Droichid	The wood of the bridge
Rossmore	An Ros Mór	The big wood
Silvermines (Eng.)	Béal Átha Gabhann	Fordmouth of the smith
Templederry	Teampall Doire	Oakgrove church
Templemore	An Teampall Mór	The big church
Templetuohy	Teampall Tuaithe	Tribal church
Terryglass	Tír dhá Ghlas	Land of two streams
Thurles	Durlas	Strong fort
Tipperary	Tiobraid Árann	Well of the Ara (river)

Munster—*Cúige Mumhan*

Toom	Tuaim	Burial mound
Toomevara	Tuaim Uí Mhéara	O'Meara's gravemound
Tour	An Tuar	The bleach green
Two Mile Borris (Eng.)	Buiríos Léith	Borough of the half

County Waterford—*Contae Phort Láirge*

Abbeyside	Dún na Mainistreach	Fort of the abbey
Aglish	An Eaglais	The church
Annestown	Bun Abha	Rivermouth
Ardmore	Aird Mhór	Great height
Ballinamult	Béal na Molt	Ford mouth of the wethers
Ballyduff	An Baile Dubh	The black town
Ballymacarberry	Baile Mhac Cairbre	Town of the sons of Cairbre
Ballymacart	Baile Mhac Airt	Town of the sons of Art
Ballymacaw	Baile Mhac Dháith	Town of the sons of Dath
Cappagh	An Cheapaigh	The plot of land
Cappoquin	Ceapach Choinn	Conn's plot
Carrickbeg	An Charraig Bheag	The little rock
Cheekpoint	Pointe na Síge	Fairy point
Clashmore	Clais Mhór	Big trench
Clonea	Cluain Fhia	Deer's Meadow
Dungarvan	Dún Garbhán	Garbhan's fort
Dunmore East	Dún Mór	Big fort
Fenor	Fionnúir	White water
Glencairn (Eng.)	Baile an Gharráin	The town of the grove
Kill	An Chill	The church
Kilmacthomas	Coill Mhic Thomáisín	Mac Thomas's wood
Kilmanahan	Cill Mainchín	St Mainchin's church
Kilmeaden	Cill Mhíodáin	St Miodan's church
Kinsalebeg (Eng.)	Baile an Phoill	The town of the hole
Knockanore	Cnoc an Oir	The hill of gold

Munster—*Cúige Mumhan*

Lackaroe	An Leaca Rua	The red flagstone
Lemybrien	Léim Uí Bhriain	O'Brien's leap
Lismore	Lios Mór	Large ringfort
Portlaw	Port Lách	Friendly fortress
Rathgormack	Ráth Ó gCormaic	O'Cormack's ringfort
Ring	An Rinn	The headland
Stradbally	An tSráidbhaile	The village
Tallow	Tulach an Iarainn	The hill of the iron
Tramore	Trá Mhór	Big strand
Villierstown (Eng.)	An Baile Nua	The new town

Ulster—*Cúige Uladh*

County Antrim—*Contae Aontroma*

Aghalee	Achadh Lí	Li's field
Ahoghill	Achadh Eochaille	Field of the yews
Antrim	Aontroim	(obs.) Single elder tree?
Armoy	Oirthear Maí	East of the plain
Artnagross	Ard na gCros	Height of the crosses
Aughafatten	Achadh Pheatan	Peatan's field
Aughagallon	Achadh Gallan	Field of the standing-stones
Ballinderry	Baile an Doire	Town of the oakgrove
Ballintoy	Baile an Tuaighe	(obs.) Town of the axe?
Ballybogey	Baile an Bhogaigh	Town of the marshy land
Ballyboyland	Baile Uí Bhaolláin	Boylan's town
Ballycarry	Baile Cora	Weir town
Ballycastle	Baile an Chaisil	The town of the stone fort
Ballyclare	Bealach Cláir	Plain road
Ballyeaston	Baile Uistín	Austin's town
Ballygally	Baile Geithligh	Geithleach's town
Ballykeel	An Baile Caol	The narrow town
Ballymaconnelly	Baile Mhic Conaíle	Connolly's town
Ballymena	An Baile Meánach	The middle town
Ballymoney	Baile Monaidh	Peat town
Ballynure	Baile an Iúir	The town of the yew
Ballyrobert	Baile Riobaird	Robert's town
Ballysillan	Baile na Saileán	Town of the osier bed
Ballyvoy	Baile Bhóidh	(obs.) Bo's town?
Balmoral	Baile Mhoireil	(obs.) Proud town?

Belfast	Béal Feirste	Mouth of the sandy ford
Broughshane	Bruach Sheáin	John's brink
Carnalbanagh	Carn Albanach	Scotsman's cairn
Carnmoney	Carn Monaidh	Peat heap
Carrickfergus	Carraig Fhearghais	Fergus's rock
Clough	An Chloch	The stone (castle)
Corkey	Corcaigh	Marsh
Craigs	Na Creaga	Outcrops
Crosskeys (Eng.)	Na hEochracha	The keys
Crumlin	Cromghlinn	Crooked glen
Culcrum	An Choill Chrom	The twisted wood
Cullybackey	Coill na Baice	The wood of the hollow
Cushendall	Bun Abhann Dalla	Mouth of the Dall (River)
Cushendun	Bun Abhann Duinne	Mouth of the Dun (River)
Dervock	Dearbhóg	(obs.) Little oak grove
Doagh	Dumhach	Dune
Drumdollagh	Droim Dallach	(obs.) Blind ridge?
Dunadry	Dún Eadradh	(obs.)Eadra's fort?
Dundrod	Dún dTrod	(obs.) Fort of the fight?
Dunloy	Dún Lathaí	(obs.)Fort of the warriors?
Dunmurry	Dún Muirígh	Murray's fort
Dunseverick	Dún Sobhairce	Sobharc's fort
Eden	An tÉadan	The brow (of the hill)
Finaghy	An Fionnachadh	White field
Finvoy	An Fionnbhoith	The white hut
Garronpoint	An Gearrán	(obs.) Cliff-edge
Glarryford	An tAth Glárach	The muddy ford
Glenard	Gleann Aird	Glen of the hillock
Glenariffe	Gleann Aireamh	Ploughmen's valley
Glenarm	Gleann Arma	(obs.)Valley of the Arm (river)
Glenavy	Lann Abhaigh	Church of the dwarf
Glenbush	Gleann na Buaise	Valley of the Bush (river)
Glenravel	Gleann Fhreabhail	(obs.)

Glenwherry	Gleann an Choire	Valley of the whirlpool
Glynn	An Gleann	The valley
Gracehill (Eng.)	Baile Uí Chinnéide	Kennedy's town
Greencastle (Eng.)	Cloch Mhic Coisteala	Costello's castle
Kells	Na Cealla	The monastic cells
Killagan	Cill Lagáin	Church of the hollow
Killans	Na Coillíní	The little woods
Killead	Cill Éad	(obs.) Hugh's church?
Killygarn	Coill na gCarn	Wood of the cairns
Kilraughts	Cill Reachtais	Church of the administration
Kilwaughter	Cill Uachtair	Church of the upperlands
Knockahollet	Cnoc an Chollait	(obs.) Hill of the heifer?
Knocknacarry	Cnoc na Cora	Hill of the weir
Lambeg	Lann Bheag	Little church
Larne	Latharna	Lahar's district
Legoniel	Lag an Aoil	Lime deposit
Lisburn (Eng.)	Lios na gCearrbhach	Ringfort of the card-players
Liscolman	Lios Cholmáin	Colman's ringfort
Lisrodden	Lios Rodáin	Ringfort of the little road
Loanends (Eng.)	Carn Mhéabha	Maeve's cairn
Loughgiel	Loch gCaol	Lake of the narrows
Magheragall	Machaire na gCeall	The plain of the churches
Magheramorne	Machaire Morna	Morna's plain
Mallusk	Maigh Bhloisce	Closkey's plain
Malone	Maigh Lón	Plain of the meadows
Moneyglass	An Muine Glas	The grey plain
Moneynick	Muine Chnoic	Hill thicket
Moyarget	Maigh Airgid	Silver plain
Muckamore	Maigh Chomair	Plain of the confluence
Parkmore	An Pháirc Mhór	The big field
Pharis	Fáras	Habitation
Port Ballintrae	Port Bhaile an Trá	Harbour of the town of the strand
Portglenone	Port Chluain Eoghain	The fort of Eoghan's meadow

Portrush	Port Rois	Headland harbour
Rasharkin	Ros Earcáin	Earcan's wood
Rathcoole	Ráth Cúile	Cul's ringfort
Rathkenny	Ráth Cheinnigh	Ceannach's ringfort
Rathlin	Reachlainn	(obs.)
Skegoneill	Sceitheog an Iarla	Shield of the earl
Straid	An tSráid	The street
Stranocum	Sraith Nócam	Nocam's spreading-ground
Templepatrick	Teampall Phádraig	St Patrick's Church
Turreagh	An Torr Riabhach	The striped rock

County Armagh—*Contae Ard Mhacha*

Aghacommon	Achadh Camán	Hurley field
Ahorey	Áth Óraí	(obs.) Gilded ford?
Allistragh	An tAileastrach	(obs.) Place of wild irises?
Altnamachin	Alt na Meacan	(obs.) The steep glen of the tubers?
Annaghmore	Eanach Mór	Great marsh
Armagh	Ard Mhacha	Macha's height
Ballsmill	Baile na gCléireach	The town of the clerks
Ballynacorr	Baile na Cora	The town of the weir
Battlehill (Eng)	An Céide Mór	The large flat-topped hill
Belleeks	Béal Leice	The fordmouth of the flagstone
Blackwatertown (Eng.)	An Port Mór	The large harbour
Camlough	Camloch	Crooked lake
Carnagh	Carranach	(obs.) Place of heaps?
Clontigora	Cluainte Gabhra	Goat meadows
Cloughoge	Clochóg	Stony place
Collone	Call Lóin	Hazelwood
Crossmaglen	Crois Mhic Lionnáin	Mac Lionnan's Cross
Cullyhanna	Coilleach Eanach	(obs.) Woody marshland?
Darkley	Dearclaigh	(obs.) Observation point?
Derryadd	Doire Fhada	Long oakgrove
Derryanville	Doire Chanabhail	(obs.) Conville's oakgrove?
Derryhaw	Doire an Chatha	Oakgrove of the battle
Derrykeevan	Doire Chaomhaín	Kevin's oakgrove

Derrylee	Doire Lí	Li's oakgrove
Derrynoose	Doire Núis	Oakgrove of the beestings
Derrytrasna	Doire Trasna	Oakgrove on the other side
Drumannon	Droim Meannáin	Kid ridge
Drumantee	Dromainn Tí	Mound of the house
Forkhill	Foirceal	(obs.) Boundary?
Jonesborough (Eng.)	Baile an Chláir	Town of the plain
Keady	An Céide	The plateau
Killeavy	Cill Shléibhe	Mountain church
Killycomain	Coill Mhic Giolla Mhaoil	Wood of the son of the bald servant
Killylea	Coillidh Léith	Grey wood
Kilmore	An Chill Mhór	The big church
Knocknamuckly	Cnoc na Muclaí	(obs.) Hill of pigs?
Laurelvale (Eng.)	Tamhnaigh Bhealtaine	(obs.)The May grasslands?
Lislea	Lios Liath	Grey fort
Lisnadill	Lios na Daille	Fort of blindness
Loughgall	Loch gCál	(obs.) Lake of need?
Loughgilly	Loch Goilí	(obs.) Lake of weeping?
Lurgan	An Lorgain	The strip of land
Middletown (Eng.)	Coillidh Chanannáin	O'Canannan's wood
Mowhan	Much Bhán	White fumes
Mullaghbawn	An Mullach Bán	The white hilltop
Portadown	Port an Dúnáin	Small fort harbour
Richhill (Eng.)	Log an Choire	Hollow of the whirlpool
Tandragee	Tóin re Gaoith	Leeside (lit. arse to wind)
Tullyrone	Tulaigh Ruáin	The hillock of the red-haired person
Tynan	Tuíneán	(obs.) Thatched place?
Woodview (Eng.)	Mullach na Saileach	The hilltop of willows

County Cavan—*Contae an Chabháin*

Ardlogher	Ard Luachra	Rushy height
Arva	Ármhach	Place of slaughter
Bailieborough	Coill an Chollaigh	The wood of the boar
Ballinagh	Béal Átha na nEach	Fordmouth of the steeds
Ballyconnell	Béal Átha Conaill	Fordmouth of Conall
Ballyhaise	Béal Átha hÉis	(obs.) Fordmouth of the cataract
Ballyheelan	Bealach an Chaoláin	The creek road
Ballyhugh	Bealach Aodha	Hugh's road
Ballyjamesduff	Baile Shéamais Dhuibh	James Duff's town
Bawnboy	An Bábhún Buí	The yellow bawn
Beglieve	Beagshliabh	Little mountain
Belturbet	Béal Tairbirt	(obs.) Mouth of the stream?
Blacklion	An Blaic	(obs.) The blossom?
Carrickaboy	Carraigigh Bhuí	(obs.) Yellow rocks?
Carrigan	An Carraigín	The little rock
Cavan	An Cabhán	The hollow
Clifferna	An Chliaifearna	(obs.) Alder-hurdle?
Cloverhil l(Eng.)	Droim Caiside	Cassidy's ridge
Cootehill	Muinchille	Sleeve
Corlesmore	Corrlios Mór	The large odd-shaped fort
Corlough	Corlach	(obs.) Twisted lake?
Cornafean	Corr na Féinne	The hill of the Fianna
Corraneary	Corr an Aoire	The shepherd's hill
Crossdoney	Cros Domhnaigh	Cross of the church

Crosserlough	Crois ar Loch	Cross on lake
Crosskeys (Eng)	Carraig an Tobair	The well rock
Crossreagh	An Chros Riabhach	The striped cross
Dernacrieve	Doire na Criadh	The clayey oakgrove
Derrylane	Doire Leathan	Wide oakgrove
Doogary	An Dúgharraí	The black garden
Dowra	An Damhshraith	(obs.) Ox-swathe?
Drumanespic	Droim an Easpaig	The bishop's ridge
Drumcask	Droim Cásca	Easter ridge
Drumeague	Droim Éag	(obs.) Death ridge?
Drung	Drong	Throng of people
Eighter	Íochtar	Bottom
Glangevlin	Gleann Ghaibhle	Glen of the fork
Glassleck	Glasleic	Grey flagstone
Grousehall (Eng.)	Maigh Leacht	Plain of the gravemound
Gubavenny	Gob an Mhianaigh	The ore promontory
Kilcogy	Cill Chóige	Coige's church
Kildorough	Coill Dorcha	Dark wood
Kill	An Chill	The church
Killeshandra	Cill na Seanrátha	(obs.) Church of the old rules?
Killinkere	Cillín Chéir	Ciar's cell
Kilmacaran	Cill Mhic Giolla Ratháin	Mac Giolla Rathan's church
Kilnaleck	Cill na Leice	The church of the flagstone
Lisboduff	Lios Bó Dubh	Black cow ringfort
Lisduff	An Lios Dubh	The black ringfort
Liscrey	Lios Cré	Clay ringfort
Lisnageer	Lios na gCaor	The ringfort of the berries
Loch Gowna	Loch Gamhna	Calf lake
Losset	An Losaid	The trough
Loughduff	An Lathaigh Dhubh	The black mud
Madabawn	An Maide Bán	The white stick
Moneygashel	Muine na gCaiseal	The thicket of the stone castles
Mountain Lodge (Eng.)	Taobh na nEas	Hillside of the cascades

Ulster—*Cúige Uladh*

Mount Nugent (Eng.)	Droichead Uí Dhálaigh	Daly's bridge
Mullagh	An Mullach	The hilltop
New Inn (Eng.)	An Dromainn	The ridge
Shercock	Searcóg	Little sweetheart
Stradone	Sraith an Domhain	Swathe of the earth
Swanlinbar (Eng.)	An Muileann Iarainn	The iron mill
Termon	An Tearmann	The sanctuary ground
Tullyco	Tulaigh Chuach	Cuckoo hills
Tullyvin	Tulaigh Bhinn	(obs.) Cliff top?
Tunnyduff	An Tonnaigh Dhubh	Black billows
Virginia (Eng.)	Achadh an Iúir	The yew field

County Derry—*Contae Dhoire*

Aghadowey	Achadh Dubhthaigh	Duffy's field
Aghanloo	Ath Lú	Lu's ford
Altmover	Alt Mómhar	Graceful deep valley
Ardgarvan	Ard Garbháin	Rough height
Ardmore	An tArd Mór	Great height
Articlave	Ard an Chléibh	The height of the basket
Ballinderry Bridge	Droichead Bhaile an Doire	The bridge of the town of the oakgrove
Ballougry	Baile Dhúdhoire	The townland of the black oakgrove
Ballykelly	Baile Uí Cheallaigh	Kelly's town
Ballymaguigan	Baile Mhic Uiginn	McGuigan's town
Ballynease	Baile Naosa	Naosa's town
Ballyronan	Baile Uí Rónáin	O'Ronan's town
Bellaghy	Baile Eachaidh	Eochaidh's town
Bellarena	Baile an Mhargaidh	The town of the market
Blackhill (Eng.)	An Mullán	The hillock
Bolea	Both Liath	Grey hut
Boveva	Boith Mhéabha	Maeve's hut
Campsie	Camsan	Short bend
Castledawson (Eng.)	An Seanmhullach	The old hilltop
Churchtown (Eng.)	Tulaigh an Iúir	The hill of the yew
Claudy	Clóidigh	Mountain streams
Cloyfin	An Chloich Fhionn	The bright stone
Coleraine	Cúil Raithin	Ferny recess

Coolkeeragh	Cúil Chaorach	Recess of the sheep
Creggan	An Creagán	The stony place
Culcrow	Cúil Chnó	Nut recess
Culmore	An Chúil Mhór	The large recess
Culnady	Cúil Chnáidí	Recess of the thistles
Curran	An Corrán	Crescent of land
Derry	Doire	Oakgrove
Derrychrier	Doire an Chriathair	Oakgrove of the sieve
Desertmartin	Díseart Mhártain	Martin's hermitage
Downhill (Eng.)	Dún Bó	Fort of the cows
Draperstown (Eng.)	Baile na Croise	Cross town
Drumahoe	Droim na hUamha	The ridge of the cave
Drumcroone	Droim Cruithean	(obs.) Ridge of wheat?
Drumraighland	Droim Raithleann	(obs.) Raithleann's ridge
Drumsurn	Droim Sorn	Ridge of the furnaces
Dungiven	Dún Geimhin	The fort of the hide
Eglington (Eng.)	An Mhagh	The plain
Fallaghloon	Folach Ghlún	(obs.) Concealment place of the generations?
Feeny	Na Fíneadha	The tribesmen
Garvagh	Garbhachadh	Rough field
Glenone	Cluain Eoghain	Eoghan's meadow
Goshaden	Geosadán	(Place of) thistles
Kilcronaghan	Cill Chruithneacháin	Cruithneachán's church
Killaloe	Coill an Lao	The wood of the calf
Killykergan	Coill Uí Chiaragáin	O'Kerrigan's wood
Kilrea	Cill Ria	(obs.) Ria's Church?
Knockcloghrim	Cnoc Clochdhroma	The hill of the stone ridge
Limavady	Léim an Mhadaidh	The dog's leap
Lislea	Lios Liath	Grey ringfort
Lisnagelvin	Lios Mhic Dhuibhleacháin	Mac Dullaghan's ringfort
Lisnamuck	Lios na Muc	The ringfort of the swine
Loup	An Lúb	The coil

Macosquin	Maigh Choscáin	Coscan's plain
Maghera	Machaire Rátha	Plain of the ringfort
Magherafelt	Machaire Fíolta	Fíolta's plain
Magilligan	Aird Mhic Giollagáin	MacGilligan's height
Mayogall	Maigh Ghuala	Plain of the shoulder
Moneydig	Muine Dige	(obs.)Thicket with ditches?
Moneymore	Muine Mór	Big thicket
Moneyneaney	Móin na nIonadh	The bog of the wonders
Muldonagh	Maol Domhnaigh	Servant of the church
Myroe	Maigh na Rua	The plain of the red-haired people
Park	An Pháirc	The field
Ringsend (Eng.)	Droichead na Carraige	Rock bridge
Shantallow	Seantalamh	Old ground
Slaughtmanus	Sleacht Mhánasa	Manus's issue
Straidarran	Sráidbhaile Uí Áráin	The village of the family of Ara
Swatragh	An Suaitreach	The (billeted) soldier
Tamlaght O'Crilly	Tamhlacht Uí Chroiligh	The grave of the Crillys
The Collon	Cuilleann	(obs.) Recessed land
Tirkane	Tír Chiana	Ciana's land
Tirmacoy	Tír Mhic Eochaidh	Mac Eochadh's land
Tobermore	An Tobar Mór	The big well
Tullintrain	Tulaigh an Tréin	The hills of the warrior
Upperlands (Eng.)	Áth an Phortáin	The ford of the cripple

County Donegal—*Contae Dhún na nGall*

Annagry	Áth na gCoire	Ford of the cauldron
Ardara	Ard an Rátha	Height of the ringfort
Arranmore	Árainn Mhór	Large sea rock
Ballinamore	Béal an Átha Móir	Mouth of the large ford
Ballindrait	Baile an Droichid	Bridgetown
Ballintra	Baile an tSratha	Town of the holm
Ballybofey	Bealach Féich	Fiach's highroad
Ballygorman	Baile Uí Ghormáin	O'Gorman's town
Ballyheerin	Baile Uí Shírín	Sheerin's town
Ballylar	Baile Láir	Centre town
Ballyliffen	Baile Lifín	(obs.) Ha'penny town?
Ballymagan	Baile Mhic Cionaoith	MacKenna's town
Ballymaleel	Baile Uí Mhaolaíola	O'Maolaiola's town
Ballynashannagh	Baile na Seanach	(obs.)
Ballyshannon	Béal Átha Seanaidh	Fordmouth of the hillside
Barnesmore	An Bearnas Mór	The great pass
Bogay	Both Ghé	Goose hut
Breenagh	Na Bruíneacha	(obs.) Place of quarrelsome people?
Brinlack	Bun na Leaca	Base of the flagstones
Bruckless	An Bhroclais	Badger sett
Bunbeg	An Bun Beag	The small river mouth
Buncrana	Bun Cranncha	Mouth of the river Crana
Bundoran	Bun Dobhráin	Mouth of the river Dobhran
Burtonport (Eng.)	Ailt an Chorráin	Ravine of the curve

Carndonagh	Carn Domhnach	Cairn of the church
Carrick	An Charraig	The rock
Carrigans	An Carraigín	The little rock
Carrigart	Carraig Airt	Art's rock
Carrowdoan	Ceathrú Domhain	The deep quarter
Carrowmena	Ceathrú Meánach	Middle quarter
Cashelmore	An Caiseal Mór	The big stone fort
Castlefin	Caisleán na Finne	Castle of the river Finn
Cavangarden	Cabhán an Gharraí	Hollow of the garden
Churchill (Eng.)	Mín an Lábáin	The level muddy place
Cloghan	An Clochán	The stepping-stones
Cloghore	Cloich Óir	Goldstone
Clonleigh	Cluain Lao	Calf meadow
Clonmany	Cluain Maine	Maine's meadow
Clontallagh	Cluain tSalach	Weedy meadow
Clooney	An Chluanaidh	The meadow
Commeen	An Coimín	Common land
Convoy	Conmhaigh	Hound plain
Coolboy	An Cúl Buí	The yellow recess
Cranford	Creamhghort	Field of garlic
Creeslough	An Craoslach	The gorge
Croagh	An Chruach	The stack
Crolly	Croithlí	(obs.) Steep way?
Culdaff	Cúil Dabhcha	(obs.) Recess of the flax-dam?
Culkeeny	Cúil Chaonaigh	Mossy recess
Derrybeg	Doirí Beaga	Little oakgroves
Doaghbeg	Dumhaigh Bhig	(Place of) the little dune
Donegal	Dún na nGall	The fort of the foreigners
Doochary	An Dúchoraidh	The black weir
Downings	Na Dúnaibh	The forts
Drimfries	Droim Fraoigh	Heather ridge
Drumkeen	Droim Caoin	Smooth ridge

Dunaff	Dún Damh	Fort of the oxen
Dunfanaghy	Dún Fionnachaidh	Fort of the white field
Dungloe		Fort of tumult
(Irish name	An Clochán Liath	The grey stepping-stones)
Dunkineely	Dún Cionnaola	Kenneally's fort
Dunlewy	Dún Lúiche	Lughdhach's fort
Fahan	Fathain (Mhura)	Sheltered place (of St Mura)
Falcarragh	An Fál Carrach	The rough edge
Fintown	Baile na Finne	Town of the (river) Finn
Frosses	Na Frosa	The showers
Glen	An Gleann	The valley
Glenagivney	Gleann na gCuimhní	The glen of memories
Glencolumbkille	Gleann Cholm Cille	St Colm's valley
Glendowan	Gleann Domhain	Deep valley
Gleneely	Gleann Daoile	Daol's valley
Glenties	Na Gleannta	The valleys
Glentogher	Gleann Tóchair	The valley of the causeway
Glenvar	Gleann Bhairr	Valley of the height
Gortahork	Gort an Choirce	Oatfield
Greenans	Na Grianáin	The summerhouses
Greencastle (Eng.)	An Caisleán Nua	The new castle
Gweedore	Gaoth Dobhair	Dore inlet
Inch	An Inis	The island
Inishbofinne	Inis Bó Finne	White cow island
Inishfraoich	Inis Fraoigh	Heather island
Inishmeane	Inis Meán	Middle island
Inver	Inbhear	Estuary
Kerrykeel	An Cheathrú Chaol	The narrow quarter
Kilcar	Cill Charthaigh	St Carthach's church
Killybegs	Na Cealla Beaga	The small monastic cells
Killygordon	Cúil na gCuirridín	The recess of the equisetum
Kilmacrennan	Cill Mhic Néanáin	Church of the son of Neanan
Kilraine	Cill Riáin	St Rian's church

Kincasslagh	Cionn Caslach	Creek head
Kindrum	Cionn Droma	Head of the ridge
Knockbrack	An Cnoc Breac	The speckled hill
Laghey	An Lathaigh	The muddy place
Lecamy	Leic Éime	Eime's flagstone
Letterbarrow	Leitir Beara	Spiky hillside
Letterkenny	Leitir Ceanainn	(obs.) Ceanann's hillside
Lettermacaward	Leitir Mhic an Bhaird	Hillside of the son of the bard
Lifford	Leifear	(obs.)
Linsfort	Lios Loinn	Lonn's fort
Loughros Point	Luacharos	(obs.) Rushy head?
Maghery	An Machaire	The plain
Malin	Málainn	(obs.) Hill-brow?
Malin Beg	Málainn Bhig	Small hill-brow
Malinmore	Málainn Mhóir	Large hill-brow
Meenacross	Mín na Croise	The level place of the cross
Meenaneary	Mín an Aoire	The level place of the shepherd
Meenbanad	Mín Beannaid	The level place of the habitation
Meenlaragh	Mín Lárach	The level place of the mare
Milford (Eng.)	Baile na nGallóglach	Town of the gallowglasses
Mountcharles	Moin Séarlais	Charles's bog
Moville	Maigh Bhile	Plain of the tree
(Irish name	Bun an Phobail	The end of the parish)
Muff	Magh	Plain
Cruit	Oiléan Cruite	Harp
Gabhla	Oileán Gabhla	(obs.)
Uaigh	Oileán Uaighe	Grave
Pettigo	Paiteagó	(obs.) Place of the smith's house?
Portnablagh	Port na Bláiche	The harbour of the buttermilk
Portnoo	Port Nua	New harbour
Portsalon	Port an tSalainn	The harbour of the salt
Ramelton	Ráth Mealtain	Mealtan's ringfort

Ranafast	Rinn na Feirste	Spit of the sandy inlet
Raphoe	Ráth Bhoth	Hut ringfort
Rathmullen	Ráth Maoláin	Maolan's ringfort
Ray	An Ráith	The ringfort
Rosbeg	Ros Beag	Little headland
Rossnakill	Ros na Cille	The headland of the church
Rossnowlagh	Ros Neamhlach	Unfriendly headland
Shrove	An tSrúibh	The stream
Speenogue	Spíonóg	Gooseberry
Stranorlar	Srath an Urláir	The holm of the floor
Tamney	An Tamhnaigh	The green place
Teelin	Teileann	(obs.)
Termon	An Tearmann	The sanctuary land
Tievemore	Taobh Mór	Large (hill)side
Tory Island	Toraigh	Place of towers
Ture	An tIúr	The yew-tree

County Down—*Contae an Dúin*

Annaclone	Eanach Cluana	Meadow marsh
Annacloy	Áth na Cloiche	The ford of the stone
Annahilt	Eanach Eilte	Doe marsh
Annalong	Áth na Long	The ford of the ships
Ardaragh	Ard Darach	Oak height
Ardenlee	Ardán Liath	Grey terrace
Ardglass	Ard Ghlais	Glas's height
Ardkeen	Ard Caoin	Pleasant height
Attical	Áit Tí Chathail	Place of Cathal's house
Ballee	Béal la	(obs.) Island mouth?
Ballinaskeagh	Baile na Sceach	The town of the hawthorn
Ballinran	Baile an Raithin	The town of the fern
Ballyalton	Baile Altúin	(obs.) Town of the ravine?
Ballyardle	Baile Ardghail	Ardghal's town
Ballyaughlis	Baile na hEachlaisce	The town of the horsewhip
Ballyculter	Baile Uí Choltair	Coulter's town
Ballydugan	Baile Uí Dhúgáin	Dougan's town
Ballygowan	Baile Mhic Gabhann	Smith's town
Ballygrainey	Baile na Gréine	The town of the sun
Ballyhackamore	Baile Hacamar	(obs.)
Ballyhornan	Baile Uí Chornáin	Hornan's town
Ballykillbeg	Baile na gCeall Beag	Town of the little cells
Ballykinlar	Baile Coinnleora	Candlestick town
Ballymacarret	Baile Mhic Gearóid	Gerard's town
Ballynabragget	Baile na Brogóide	Town of the malt

Ulster—*Cúige Uladh*

Ballynafeigh	Baile na Faiche	Town of the green
Ballynagarrick	Baile na gCarraig	Town of the rocks
Ballynahinch	Baile na hInse	Town of the holm
Ballyroney	Baile Uí Ruanaí	Rooney's town
Ballysallough	Baile Salach	Town of the osiers
Bangor	Beannchar	(obs.) (Place of) pointed hills?
Blackskull (Eng.)	Baile Mhic Dhonnagáin	Town of the son of Donegan
Bright	Breachtán	(obs.) Magic charm?
Burren	Boirinn	(obs.) Stony place?
Cabra	An Chabrach	The poor land
Carrowdore	Ceathrú Dobhair	Water quarter
Carryduff	Ceathrú Aodha Dhuibh	Black Hugh's quarter
Castlewellan	Caisleán Uidhilín	Whelan's castle
Clandeboye	Clann Aodha Buí	(Land of) the family of Aodh Boy
Clare	An Clár	The plain
Clough	An Chloch	The stone
Cloughey	Clochaigh	Stony place
Comber	An Comar	The confluence
Conlig	An Choinleic	The flagstone of the hounds
Craigavad	Creig an Bháda	The town of the boat
Cregagh	An Chreagaigh	The stony place
Crossgar	An Chrois Ghearr	The short cross
Dechomet	Deachoimheád	(Obs.) Secure guard?
Derryboy	Doire Buí	Yellow oakgrove
Donaghadee	Domhnach Daoi	Daoi's church
Donaghcloney	Domhnach Cluana	Church of the meadow
Donaghmore	Domhnach Mór	Big church
Downpatrick	Dún Pádraig	St Patrick's fort
Dromara	Droim Bearach	Ridge of heifers
Dromore	Droim Mór	Large ridge
Drumaness	Droim an Easa	The ridge of the cascade
Drumaroad	Droim an Róid	The ridge of the road
Drumgath	Droim Ga	Spear ridge

Drumlee	Droim Lao	Calf ridge
Drumnabreeze	Droimne Bríos	(obs.) Brios's ridge?
Dundonald	Dún Dónaill	Daniel's fort
Dundrum	Dún Droma	Fort of the ridge
Dunmore	Dún Mór	Big fort
Edenderry	Éadan Doire	Hill-brow of the oakridge
Edentrillick	Éadan Trilic	(obs.) Hill-brow of the trill?
Garvaghy	Garbhachadh	Rough field
Glassdrummond	An Ghlasdromainn	The grey mound
Gransha	An Ghráinseach	The grange
Hillsborough (Eng.)	Cromghlinn	Crooked glen
Hilltown	Baile Hill	Hill's town
Holywood (Eng.)	Ard Mhic Nasca	Height of Nasca's town
Kilcoo	Cill Chua	Cua's church
Kilfullert	Coill Fulachta	Wood of the cooking-pot
Kilkeel	Cill Chaoil	Church of the narrow
Killinchy	Cill Dhuinsí	St Duinseach's church
Killough	Cill Locha	Lake Church
Killowen	Cill Eoin	Eoin's church
Killyleagh	Cill O Laoch	O'Laoch's church
Kilmore	An Chill Mhór	The big church
Kinallen	An Cionn Álainn	The lovely head
Kircubbin	Cill Ghobáin	St Goban's church
Knock	An Cnoc	The hill
Leggamaddy	Lag an Mhadaidh	Place of the dog
Leitrim	Liatroim	Grey ridge
Lenaderg	Láithreach Deirce	Ruin of the berry
Lisbane	An Lios Bán	The white ruin
Lisnacree	Lios na Crí	Boundary ringfort
Lisnastrean	Lios na Srian	Bridle ringfort
Listooder	Lios an tSúdaire	The ringfort of the tanner
Loughbrickland	Loch Bricleann	(Obs.) Bricriú's lake
Loughinisland	Loch an Oileáin	Island lake

Magheralin	Machaire Lainne	Plain of the church
The Maze	An Mhaigh	The plain
Moira	Maigh Rath	(obs.) Plain of the gifts?
Moneyrea	Monadh Riabhach	Striped bog
Moyallon	Maigh Alúine	Plain of yellow clay
Newry	An tIúr	The yew-tree
Newtownards	Baile Nua na hArda	New town of the height
Newtownbreda	Baile Nua na Bréadaí	New town of the rein
Portaferry	Port an Pheire	Harbour of the pair (the two towns)
Portavogie	Port an Bhogaigh	The harbour of the swamp
Raholp	Ráth Cholpa	Ringfort of the grazing -land
Rathfriland	Ráth Fraoileann	Fraoile's ringfort
Ravarnett	Ráth Bhearnait	Barnett's ringfort
Rostrevor	Ros Treabhair	Trevor's wood
Rubane	Rú Bán	(obs.) White rue?
Scaddy	Sceadaigh	(obs.) Brindled animals
Scarva	Scarbhach	Shallow
Scrabo	Screabach	Rough land
Seaforde	Baile Forda	Ford's town
Strangford (Eng.)	Baile Loch Cuan	The town of the lough of the safe harbour
Toghblane	Teach Bhláin	Blan's house
Toye	An Tuaith	The tribe

County Fermanagh—*Contae Fhear Manach*

Aghalane	Achadh Leathan	Broad field
Ballinamallard	Béal Átha na Mallacht	Fordmouth of the curses
Ballindarragh	Baile na Dara	Town of the oaks
Ballycassidy	Baile Uí Chaiside	Cassidy's town
Belcoo	Béal Cú	Mouth of the narrow neck
Bellanaleck	Bealach na Leice	The road of the flagstone
Belleek	Béal Leice	Fordmouth of the flagstone
Blaney	Bléinigh	Narrow tongue of land
Boa Island	Inis Badhbha	Badhbha's island
Boho	Botha	Huts
Brookeborough (Eng.)	Achadh Lon	Field of blackbirds
Church Hill (Eng.)	An Droim Meánach	The middle ridge
Clabby	Clabaigh	Open place
Coa	An Cuach	The bowl
Cooneen	An Cúinnín	Little corner
Cornafanog	Corr na bhFeannóg	The hollow of the hooded crows
Corranny	Corr Eanaigh	The marshy hollow
Creagh	Créach	Clayey place
Culkey	Cuilcigh	Rascals
Derrygonnelly	Doire Ó gConaíle	The oakgrove of the O'Connollys
Derryharney	Doire Charna	Oakgrove of flesh
Derrylester	Doire an Leastair	The oakgrove of the vessel
Derrylin	Doire Loinn	Church oakgrove
Drumcose	Droim Cuas	Cavity ridge

Drummully	Droim Ailí	Rocky ridge
Drumskinny	Droim Scine	Knife ridge
Ederney	Eadarnaidh	(obs.) Ambush?
Enniskillen	Inis Ceithleann	Ceithle's island
Esnadarra	Ais na Darach	(obs.) Place of oaks?
Five points (Eng.)	An Scéith	The shield
Florence Court (Eng.)	Mullach na Seangán	The hilltop of the ants
Garvery	Garbhaire	Rough land
Imeroo	Ime Rú	(obs.) Rue dam?
Kesh	An Cheis	The wicker causeway
Killadeas	Cill Chéile Dé	The Culdees' Church
Kilturk	Coill Torc	Boar wood
Kinawley	Cill Náile	Naile's Church
Knockaraven	Cnoc an Riabháin	Hill of the oyster-catcher
Lack	An Leac	The flagstone
Leggs	Na Laig	The hollows
Letter	An Leitir	The hillside
Letterbreen	Leitir Bhruín	Fairy-hostel hillside
Lisbellaw	Lios Béal Átha	Fordmouth ringfort
Lisnarick	Lios na nDaróg	The ringfort of the small oaks
Lisnaskea	Lios na Scéithe	The ford of the shield
Magheraveely	Machaire Mhílic	Milic's plain
Monea	Maigh Niadh	Warrior plain
Roscor	Ros Corr	Twisted wood
Roslea	Ros Liath	Grey wood
Scribbagh	Scriobach	Scratchy ground
Stragolan	Srath Gabhláin	Creek holm
Tamlaght	Tamhlacht	Grave
Tempo	An tIompú Deiseal	The right turn
Tullyhommon	Tulaigh Uí Thiomáin	O'Tioman's hillocks
Tullyrosmearn	Tulaigh Ros Sméarann	Blackberry wood hillocks
Whitehill (Eng.)	Tír Uí Bhranáin	Brandon's land

County Monaghan—*Contae Mhuineacháin*

Aghabog	Achadh Bog	Soft field
Anyalla	Eanaigh Gheala	Bright marshes
Aughnamullen	Achadh na Muileann	Field of the mills
Ballinode	Béal Átha an Fhóid	Fordmouth of the sod
Ballybay	Béal Átha Beithe	Fordmouth of the birch
Balymackney	Baile Macnaí	MacNee's town
Bradox	Na Bráideoga	(obs.) Child's bibs?
Brandrum	Bréandroim	Slope of the ridge
Carrickmacross	Carraig Mhachaire Rois	The rock of the plain of Ross
Carrickroe	An Charraig Rua	The red rock
Castleblayney (Eng.)	Baile na Lorgan	Town of the land-strip
Clones	Cluain Eois	The meadow of Eos
Clontibret	Cluain Tiobrad	Well meadow
Coolderry	Cúl Doire	Oakgrove recess
Corduff	An Chorr Dhubh	The black hill
Cortubber	Corr Tobair	Well hill
Creighanroe	Crícheán Rua	(obs.) Small red bush?
Dartry	Dartraí	(obs.) Oak holm?
Donaghmoyne	Domnach Maighean	Church steading
Doohamlet	Dúthamhlacht	Black graveyard
Doohat	Dútháite	Black "tate" (Old land measure = 60 Irish acres)
Drum	An Droim	The ridge
Drumacrib	Droim Mhic Roib	Robson's ridge
Drumakill	Droim na Coille	The ridge of the wood

Dunraymond	Dún Réamainn	Redmond's fort
Emyvale	Scairbh na gCaorach	The shallow of the sheep
Glaslough	Glasloch	Grey lake
Inniskeen	Inis Caoin	Pleasant island
Killybrone	Coillidh Brón	Wood of sorrows
Knockatallon	Cnoc an tSalainn	The hill of the salt
Laragh	Láithreach	Site
Latnamard	Leacht na mBard	The gravemound of the poets
Latton	Leatón	(obs.) Half-base?
Lisnalong	Lios na Long	The ringfort of the ships
Loughmorne	Loch Morn	(obs.) Morna's lake
Magheracloone	Machaire Cluana	Plain of the meadow
Monaghan	Muineachán	Place of thickets
Mullan	An Muileann	The mill
Newbliss (Eng.)	Cúil Darach	Oak recess
Rockcorry	Buíochar	(obs.) Yellow edge?
Selloo	Suí Lú	Lú's place
Shantonagh	Seantonnach	Old quagmire
Smithborough (Eng.)	Na Mullaí	The heights
Stranooden	Sraith Nuadáin	Nuada's holm
Swan's Cross Roads (Eng.)	An Droim Mór	The big ridge
Tydavnet	Tigh Damhnata	St Davnet's church

County Tyrone—*Contae Thír Eoghain*

Aghyaran	Achadh Uí Áráin	The field of the family of Ara
Altamuskin	Alt na Múscán	The ravine of the sponges
Altishahane	Alt Inse Uí Chatháin	The ravine of O'Kane's holm
Arboe	Ard Bó	Cow height
Ardstraw	Ard Sratha	Holm height
Ardtrea	Ard Tré	(obs.) Height of the spear?
Artigarvan	Ard Tí Garbháin	The height of Garbhan's house
Aughamullen	Achadh Uí Mhaoláin	Mullen's field
Augher	Eochair	Border
Aughintain	Achadh an tSéin	Field of the fairy fort
Aughnacloy	Achadh na Cloiche	The field of the stone
Ballygawley	Baile Uí Dhálaigh	Daly's town
Ballymagorry	Baile Mhic Gofraidh	MacGorry's town
Ballyneaner	Baile an Aonfhir	(obs.) Individual's town?
Benburb	An Bhinn Bhorb	The rough peak
Beragh	Bearach	(obs.) Muzzle?
Brantry	An Bréantar	(obs.) The broken lea?
Bready	An Bhréadaigh	The rein
Broughderg	Bruach Dearg	Red edge
Cabragh	An Chabrach	Copse
Caledon (Eng.)	Cionn Aird	High head
Campsie	Camsan	Short bend
Cappagh	An Cheapóg	The seed-bed
Carland	Domhnach Carr	Carr's church
Carnteel	Carn tSiail	Sial's cairn

Carrickmore	An Charraig Mhór	The big rock
Castlecaulfield (Eng.)	Baile Uí Dhonnaíle	Donnelly's town
Castlederg	Caisleán na Deirge	Castle of the Derg (River)
Clanabogan	Cluain Uí Bhogáin	Bogan's land
Clare	An Clár	The plain
Clogher	Clochar	Stony place
Clonoe	Cluain Eo	Yew meadow
Coagh	An Cuach	The hollow
Cookstown	An Chorr Chríochach	The boundary hill
Corbo	Corr Bhó	Cow hill
Cranagh	An Chrannóg	The lake dwelling
Creggan	An Creagán	The stony place
Crilly	Crithligh	Shaking bog
Cullion	Cuilleann	Holly
Curr	An Chorr	The hill
Derryfubble	Doire an Phobail	The oakgrove of the parish
Donaghanie	Domhnach an Eich	The church of the steed
Donaghey	Dún Eachaidh	(obs.) Steed castle?
Donaghmore	Domhnach Mór	Big church
Dooish	Dubhais	Black hill
Dromore	An Droim Mór	The big ridge
Drumaney	Droim Eanaigh	Marsh ridge
Drumlea	Droim Léith	Grey ridge
Drumlegagh	Droim Liagach	Stony ridge
Drumnakilly	Droim na Coille	The ridge of the wood
Drumquin	Droim Caoin	Pleasant ridge
Dunamanagh	Dún na Manach	Fort of the monks
Dungannon	Dún Geanainn	Geanann's fort
Dunmoyle	An Dún Maol	The smooth fort
Dunnamore	Domhnach Mór	Big church
Dyan	An Daighean	The fortress
Edendork	Éadan na dTorc	The hill-brow of the boars
Eglish	An Eaglais	The church

Eskra	Eiscreach	Place of eskers
Favor Royal (Eng.)	Achadh Maoil	Field of the rounded hillock
Fintona	Fionntamhnach	Fair field
Fivemiletown (Eng.)	Baile na Lorgan	Town of the shank
Fyfin	Faiche fionn	Bright green patch
Galbally	Gallbhuaile	(obs.) Town of the foreigner?
Garvaghey	Garbhachadh	Rough field
Glenhull	Gleann Choll	Valley of woods
Gortaclare	Gort an Chláir	The field of the plain
Gortavoy	Gort an Bheathaigh	The field of the cattle
Gorticastle	Gort an Chaisil	The field of the stone fort
Gortin	An Goirtín	The little field
Gortreagh	An Gort Riabhach	The striped field
Granville (Eng.)	An Doire Mhín	The level oakgrove
Killeeshill	Cill Íseal	Low church
Killen	Cillín	Little church
Killeter	Coill Íochtair	Church of the low place
Killycolpy	Coill an Cholpa	The wood of the steer
Killyman	Cill na mBan	The women's church
Kilsally	Coill Sailí	Willow wood
Kilskeery	Cill Scíre	Scíre's church
Knockmoyle	An Cnoc Maol	The rounded hill
Knocknahorn	Cnoc na hEorna	Barley hill
Leglands	Leithgleann	(obs.) Valley of the half?
Liscloon	Lios Claon	Sloping ringfort
Lisdoart	Lios Dubhairt	Dooart's ringfort
Lislap	Lios Leapa	Ringfort of the bed
Lissan	Leasán	Little ringfort
Loughmacrory	Loch Mhic Ruairi	McRory's lake
Mournebeg	An Mhorn Bheag	(obs.) Little dish?
Moy	An Maigh	The plain
Moygashel	Maigh gCaisil	Plain of stone forts
Mullaslin	Mullach Slinne	Shingly top

Munterbyrne	Muintir Bhirn	(obs.) The Bearn country?
Omagh	An Omaigh	The virgin plain
Oritor (Eng.)	Na Coracha Beaga	The little weirs
Seskanore	Seisceann Odhar	Dull-coloured bog
Seskilgreen	Seisíoch Chill Ghrianna	The sixth [land-measure] of Grianna's church
Sheskinshule	Seisceann Siúil	Weird bog
Sixmilecross (Eng.)	Na Coracha Móra	The big weirs
Stewartstown (Eng.)	An Chraobh	The branch
Strabane	An tSrath Bán	The white holm
Stralongford	Srath Longfoirt	Fortress holm
Stranagalwilly	Sraith na Gallbhuaile	Holm of the foreigners' milking-place
Tamnamore	An Tamhnach Mhór	The large green place
Tattyreagh	An Táite Riabhach	The striped 'tate' [measure = 60 Irish acres]
Tiroony	Tír Uaithne	Union land
Trillick	Trileac	Three flagstones
Tullyhogue	Tulaigh Og	Hillocks of the young
Tulnacross	Tulach na Croise	The hillock of the cross
Urney	An Urnaí	The oratory

The Poolbeg Golden Treasury of Well-Loved Poems

compiled by
Sean McMahon

A delightful anthology of classic poetry

POOLBEG

The Poolbeg Book of Children's Verse

compiled by
Sean McMahon

"Already a classic."
RTE Guide

POOLBEG

Shoes and Ships and Sealing-Wax
A Book of Quotations for Children

compiled by
Sean McMahon

A collection to amuse, surprise and delight.

POOLBEG